HEALING PRESENCE

AWARENESS OF INTERPATHIC UPLIFT

ALEX MATHEW

WestBow Press books may be ordered through booksellers or by contacting:

WestBow Press
A Division of Thomas Nelson & Zondervan
1663 Liberty Drive
Bloomington, IN 47403
www.westbowpress.com
844-714-3454

ISBN: 979-8-3850-1832-1 (sc)
ISBN: 979-8-3850-1833-8 (e)

Library of Congress Control Number: 2024902336

Print information available on the last page.

WestBow Press rev. date: 02/29/2024

DEDICATION

This book is dedicated to Dr. Anupama G., the Oncologist in Lakeshore hospital who, lovingly, interpathically showed me the possibilities in being a Healing Presence. She is an epitome of a Blessing Being in the Scriptural and practical sense of the word Blessing, which she was throughout my tryst with Multiple Myeloma, in 2016 to 2018. She is a conduit of Healing and Blessing in heavenly Grace

CONTENT

(Being a Botanist, Chapters are: Termed; Petals)

INTRODUCING THIS FRAGRANT FLOWER GIFTED TO US IN HIS GRACE

Healing presence or A Blessing Being or Christian-Meta-love counseling, Interpathic Uplift; interchangeably used in this work is an act of Christian love. This book is written in a theistic context; as I believe, God is in control of all that 'is'. It is not an easy proposition to Artificial-intelligent, technical and scientific thinking AI, ML Robotic brains. I crave forgiveness from them; not for my firm belief, but for thinking they may not be with me. Nothing for me is even indirectly indicative of a Godless existence. Existence itself is the Love-Truth that infills and surrounds all that exists, I mean the all-inclusive - 'IS'. Existence is a present-continuous-ongoing-event that can only be represented by 'IS' or as the present-continuous-state-of-being. The idea of Meta-love- counseling or A BLESSING BEING', A Healing Presence" is, being-in-the-moment-that-reveals-itself to the one who is ready in sensitive alertness to receive whatever 'IS'.

We are not entitled to alter the perpetual 'IS', which keeps changing despite our agreement or otherwise. We want, we insist and endeavor for changes as we desire. Hakuna Matata! (No problem!) But it will be hugely beneficial if we do not forget the fact that manipulating to alter it is a peculiarly particular human trait. But our definition of Meta-love-counseling or a Blessing Being, simply means the counselor remains a *'Healing Presence'* throughout the counseling process,

The word 'counselor' as a helper, healer and comforter was first mentioned by Jesus, very plainly in simple understandable form in the Gospel according to[1] John in chapter 14: 15-17. The term 'Councilor and Counselor' were very much in use even before the time of Jesus. Those counselors/counselors were parts of the official setups who wielded authority and influence.

The 'Counselor' as Jesus meant will lead you into situations that redeem and heal.

The idea is very simple.

The person, who desires to be a helper to anyone in trouble, brokenness and pain, is to be fully present with the person in pain and be led by Love and whatever the Spirit prompts that person to be. By being fully present, the contention is that the attending person needs to totally attend to the needy with all faculties namely; body, mind and spirit. No other considerations should deter the attending person from devoting completely to the needy person. Easier said than done! Then the counselor turns out to be the inlet of comfort and healing, which indeed flows from the Holy Spirit through that person who remains a pulsating conduit of healing and a source of comfort. This book is in line with my earlier books 'Beyond Techniques' and 'Making of a Christian Counselor'; *Authentic Books 2008.* You will simply be surprised at the simplicity of the meta-love-counseling process when you take a step beyond the ordinary understanding of what we mean by 'Counseling' and even Christian varieties of counseling.

Being a Healing Presence is very much a Christ-like act deeply rooted in His grace.

The Holy Spirit; source of all comfort and healing begins flowing to the person in need, through you, who functions as a genuine conduit for the happening, healing process. It may sound impractical and superstitious, but that is the simple truth, just as the wind blows and clears the air. It is a spiritual experiential, predictable, empirically demonstrable, observable truth. There is no quote from sources; which are ignorable, dispensable for those who cannot agree with the Scriptural evidences with Scriptural truth. Please be not led to think it is some religious stuff to deter people from their faiths. It is all about comforting and healing the whole person; in Spirit, Mind and Body.

No extraneous considerations influence the Meta-love-counselor in the Healing Presence.

The dynamics of such happenings is not explainable technically; as it is there, for anyone in 'whole' to experience it and for those outside it to reject it outright.

Meta-love-counseling is meta-cognitive; that is, 'the-beyond-counseling-state-of-the-ordinary' and is also beyond knowledge because it is revelational in character. Interpathic, existential, transference of divine healing to the paining and broken individuals based simply on the love of God bringing in observable transcendence. In every star of the sky and in every grain of sand and every atom that is in between, one can; if one cares to, witness the divine glow of *'The Presence'*. In all honesty some may not be able to see or even visualize it. If one does not sense it; that is perfectly normal. It only means that they do want to see and be aware that the possibility exists. Meta-love-counseling or a Blessing Being, is only possible for those who think that they do not know everything and have all the answers in their knowledge bank. Getting equipped and enabled as a Meta-love-counselor or being a 'Healing Presence' is the tough part. Once that happens, you will be used in consonance with the 'Love-truth'; the divine purpose for which all humans are called but not all are heading.

Meta-love-counseling of a Blessing Being is operative on the unalterable fact of the, Omnipresence (present everywhere), Omniactive (present in all actions), Omnimorphic (present in all forms), Omniscient (all knowing), Omni benedictio (blessing all), of the Omnipotent (all powerful), Omni phonic (present in all sounds), Omni luminous (in all lights), Omni-Omni (all and in all) God; all around and within us. A sharpened awareness of that 'Presence' is essential in Meta-love-counseling or A healing Presence. To sharpen that awareness of the Presence, the Meta-love-counselor has to learn to slip into silence that penetrate the whole being of the Meta-love-counselor making her/him vibrantly attuned to the 'Presence'. It calls for all the faculties of the Meta-love-counselor (Body, Mind and Spirit) to be at one with the Love-Truth around her/him. The mode of being in onement with Love-Truth is not a quick fix but a process that needs to be accomplished with patience and commitment in all humility. This is not some esoteric misinforming to wean people away from any other form of counseling methodologies.

- We need to concede that creation does not conform to our dispositions.
- Meta-love-counseling does not conform to our propositions or presuppositions.
- Meta-love-counseling does not conform to our preferences.
- One predisposition in Meta-love-counseling is "God is Truth, Love and Life".
- The emphatic proposition in Meta-love-counseling is 'Abide in His Love'.
- The uniquely desirable distinction in Meta-love-counseling is "Christ in me '.
- Meta-love- counseling is an act of Christ's comforting, healing love happening through the Meta-love-counselor as a Healing Presence in His glorious Presence.

Love of Christ is the active principle in Meta-love-counseling. Met-love-counseling is Christ Jesus using the counselor in His love for comforting others in interpathic (trans- empathetic) resonance. A loveless person does not make a counselor; whatever the school or system of counseling that person may have undergone. Without love, there is no positive outcome in any form of counseling. (Period)

Therapies of all descriptions may thrive even in love less deserts of technological wilderness. The truth is; no manner of counseling can ever take place in an arid atmosphere devoid of love. Without love, the counselee will only be influenced to believe everything is bound to be fine.

Love-Truth makes all things possible including all comforting, healing and wholeness. Surrounded by Love-Truth, all things become possible. Surrender in Love-Truth to sense the magic of love. Love-Truth never fails the giver or the receiver; only opens the path to enlightened understanding and positive growth.

You would not have chosen to read this book on Blessing Being/'Healing Presence' or 'Meta-love-counseling' unless you have a loving, humble, compassionate heart. You love others and you are someone with love for others in your heart. I am sure you love others because you experience the Love-Truth that is Christ and feel comfortably joyful in pouring it out for others. Perhaps you experience the love of Christ Jesus without realizing it; it does not discriminate. His love is free and free for all. Love-Truth is not compartmentalized for any particular section of humanity. People with distorted vision only see the love of Christ as reserved for their particular group. Such are the ones who degrade Love and have no understanding of the meaning and content of the Love-Truth which is Christ.

It does make no difference. Love-Truth outlasts all ludicrous claims to demean it. We know and believe that Jesus Christ is Love. He is the only one who makes sure that any Meta-love-counseling done in love is done on His behalf, through Him and by Him because His love constrains us, as He is Love. This makes it very simple and clear. The outcome of Meta-love-counseling or 'Healing Presence' is Christ's prerogative and the ideal Meta-love-counselor is only a sharpened tool in His hands. There is no room for any other pretensions or claims.

There is goodness and mercy inherent in your heart and therefore you care for people. Somewhere within you, dwells the Love that yearns to reach out. As an older person and as someone with a calling for helping others, I want to share with you what I have learned in this ministry for over five decades. I dare to do this because I am convinced it will in some way benefit you and help to fulfill your calling to be a blessing to others. Your heart is constrained by the Love of Christ to reach out to those who are in all sorts of pain. This is not an easy task. It takes a lot of determination and disarming commitment to be doing such a godly service.

People like you who venture into this field are sensitive and are readily touched and pained by the sufferings of others in an interpathic mode. This quality of the heart is an asset in counseling in the name of Jesus Christ, filled with His spirit. At the same time, you also have the weakness to be hurt easily and run the risk of over identifying with people in trouble. While you have firm faith in Christ Jesus; the embodiment of love, you also are eager to get something consummated for others. You would like to do that rather fast, in your own time and turn, and in your best judgment. This is nothing surprising as it is a very human inclination, but it often does not happen the way you want or plan.

Nothing happens according to a timetable we make ready for God.

He knows better.

You have to acknowledge that fact as a living fact. If we have the ears to hear and eyes to see and hearts to receive in ways acceptable to Him, leading will come to us in unexplained ways. A life rooted in the Word of God is the secret; a life yielding the fruit of the Spirit. That is the hard part for our kind. We unwittingly demand and expect things to happen in our ways and schedules.

This seems normal to us, but unlikely because we do not have the mandate to play God.

In counseling and in all people-helping ministries this is a natural tendency in people involved in the act of helping in Meta-love-counseling needs to be seen as an act of love because it indeed is an act of love. Through human beings as the vehicles, this ministry is made possible in the love of God.

That is the truth. That is the simple and unalterable truth.

Through Meta-love-counseling or in the Healing presence, people in trouble and pain are led to receive tangible peace and a degree of lasting joy. They are strengthened to cope with their life situations. At times, you may feel so deeply influenced by the painful circumstances of the people you try to help and you would be in a hurry to push through for desired and projected or expected results. That is where you might be tempted to get into immature and ill-considered shortcuts.

That is when you may be tempted to try some shortcuts through seemingly effective techniques. Techniques to manipulate people reduce men to mere inanimate objects or perhaps to animals without a spirit.

There is also another sad fact we need to admit. Most people want quick and easy changes which apparently would look satisfying. It is the easy and the quick that people desire. That too is understandable. What is hard to understand is the apparent lack of discretion in getting what is desired. Desires per se, drive people to commit rather foolish things. The point I am trying to put across to you is that as a Meta-love-counselor/ Blessing Being you need to be careful not to be driven by desires to achieve expected results in quick order. There is further complication in going beyond empathy and rising to interpathy. Empathy, we say, knows where the shoe bites but interpathy is getting into the experience of the pain of the other. The difference is that of knowing and being, that is; not just knowing the pain but bearing and being in the pain. I hope you are with me.

The intention of this book is also to discuss the many ways in which the Meta-love-counselor might go the wrong way in chasing desired results. You need not repeat the mistakes many have done and keep on doing in ignorance of the Love-Truth; the truth about this godly ministry. You must know the truth about this ministry you want to take up or already have taken up because you know only the Truth will set you free. For that you need exposure to some true pictures, revealing the various aspects of genuine Meta-love-counseling, A Blessing Being. You also need to be aware of the murky practices that happen in the name of counseling.

With time, I have come to accept the humbling fact that in counseling, many things often happen in spite of me and my lack of the grip of things.

I have specially chosen some revealing personal experiences for you to have a glimpse into the life and ministry of an elder counselor for you to discern some finer nuances of 'Meta-love-counseling/Healing Presence' successes and failures. You would discover that it is abounding grace all the way, all the time and not any personal mastery or professional excellence. The impossible takes a while, but it comes through in divine provisions, not according to our specifications. Humility, Holiness, Hope, love, patience, goodness, kindness, tolerance, faithfulness, gentleness, acceptance, self-control and Purity are needed all the time to understand the dynamics of Meta-love-healing.

You may have learned some models of counseling and perhaps may already be practicing these on a regular basis. It is natural for you to have a strong bias about what you practice. I do not want to dissuade you from doing what you consider as right. At the same time, it is important that you know what is right in the line of being a Meta-love-counselor representing Christ Jesus and his love, seen in the light of His Word. You may be right in doing what you consider right and I may be seen as wrong in what I put forward as right. In the same way, what I say about Meta-love-counseling in the light of my over 50 years of experience may have something reasonably right in it.

The issue is not who says what and who is right. There can only be one way that is true. We all must know that is the way of the Love-Truth. Only the Love-Truth will set us free to be ourselves and do the right thing. My conviction is that Truth is revealed in the Word of God, not just because I believe it with all my heart but because it simply is the Truth. My position can safely be ignored by all and by all means

I do not say this from an emotional base or from fear of any compulsion of any kind or from any prompting arising out of any subjective miraculous experience. I reckon I have faith enough to believe in the incarnate Word of God. My faith goes beyond what is ordinarily seen and considered definite requirements to observable faith. I have seen that invariably love is the operative force in any kind of counseling. There may be claims of preferred technological excellence over love in counseling. But as you dive deeper into the murky water of technological fixing of people, you are likely to come up with the truth of it all. That is why I take the privilege to say, let us go by the Word of God in doing what is the right path in the practice of Meta-love-counseling in His love. As you progress in our journey toward being a blessing to others, you would inevitably come to the realization that love is the essence of your ministry and that love emanates from Love-Truth that is resident within you. This is not a mystery; it is a simple fact that needs no authentication other than the Word of God. I say this because it is a promise from Love itself which stands beyond corroborative authentication[2] John 15:4 – 10, 26, and 27. However, we cannot ignore the frightening fact that we humans ordinarily spend 24x7 all 365 days and years for the gratification of our desires, keenly searching for our respective comfort zones. This has been happening from even before the advent of materialist consumerism where God is a dispensable commodity.

Materialist consumerism is not a new-fangled 21st century blundering. History testifies that consuming to appease personal avarice is as old as the oldest humans. Perhaps post-modern liberalism is a product of the 20th century. Even where there is altruistic self-striving towards service to others, there is latent desire to gratify the need for self-importance. We do that to gain an appearance of a smug social-do-gooder image and we have to confess that in reality, the striving is camouflaged pride and the means; by necessity devious.

There may be righteous anger in some about what I just said. I do not discard the possibility of a few genuine godly people constrained by the love of God doling out alms. Experience however, is that even religious leaders, let alone political bosses, indulge in the well-accepted practice of hoarding material possessions for personal pleasure-ends. Hypocrisy is a well-perfected art and way of life in most advanced societies, which is not found excluded from places of worship agencies. A Pharisee is not hard to be detected with his visibly pious limbic gesticulations and not so masked facial pretenses.

We see sights of government ministers wailing unremittingly on the vices of the priestly classes, yet very particularly protecting their own political bases and absolving their own leaders from all wrong doings. We see the high priests of sections of the faiths fighting their guts off to get a slice of the worldly goodies. In yet other places, the fight would be to increase membership of splinter denominations and sects. What are wielded in these pockets of faith-dealings would be some obscure practices or dogma based on insignificant faith strands twisted to denominational, sectarian advantages.

I can assure you, you have come to a point where nothing surprises you. The fact is; graft, bribing, dishonesty and corrupt manipulations are so rampant that we hardly see anyone bothering to react. An honest official trying a hand at cleaning the system will get transferred at speeds that exceed the honking behind you at traffic junctions.

What concerns us here is the practice of all sorts of counseling; the practicing of it and the prevalent emotive gene behind it. Sadly you would discern the influence of predominant social trends in demands for the popular. People at large prefer the touted, advertised and or the esoteric practices; all with strategies for personal gain. Emphasis is for excellence with speed. If there is a complying god who acts at the whims of the technician-counselor, that god will be touted even if that god is a mere anthropoid or a sheer technique.

While confessing largely, this is caused by whitewashed sepulchers among the walking dead of all faiths and Christians; the number of the living faithful is falling alarmingly. They are not able to live up to their faith in full. We fall for the intellectualizing of liberation. We contextualize liberation in its wild extremes missing the joy of living in simple faith.

That takes us to an important point for us to consider. There has always been a conflict of interest with the world and the true Church. The true Church teaches the people to love and live for others. Consider others more important than yourself. Christ capped it with saying there is only one command to keep "Love others even as I have loved you".[3] John.13: 34. Such teaching coming from the true Church does not jell with the materialist-consumerist-technologist-ethics of the post-modern world, which solidly stand for the right for self-determination for self-advancement. The world unfortunately has an upper hand in this conflict, as there are not many traces of a true Church in evidence. We see churches scramble for and factually encourage self-advancement through the secular technological ways of the world and even preaching the religion of Psychology from the pulpits.[4] Paul C. Witz; Psychology as Religion; Wm B. Eerdmans Publishing house, Michigan, 1994

Christian faith largely is revelational, in which the will of God is revealed in history and in personal lives. It unfortunately is not in step with the rational expectations of people seeking signs. The young people in particular are looking for self-fulfillment through self-actualization. Most want to boost self-esteem and in a hurry they run for it; more are happily ready to give up on cultural or moral frame-work of any description. They hanker for a feeling of liberation from the established code of conduct and traditional values which is worth celebrating with excesses. Here we find the loss of a vital Christian code of ethics; obedience. A compromised faith and outright disobedience in defiance of Christian values leave behind a rebellious population who do not hesitate to accept and honor anything that would presumably bring them cheer of some description. The world is eagerly searching that cheer or ease in a hedonistic-mode-of-being in the world. Christian faith is being looked down upon and discredited by the hedonists as an impracticable and an untenable system of values.

The measure of success is counted in terms of the visible popularity, flashy lifestyle, holy pretensions, pockets of influence, number of blind followers, bank balance and so on. Therefore, it is not surprising this large principle gets proportionately applied even in the area of counseling. The measure of counseling is successful fixing- of-problems. A big guru is reported to have said among other gaffe, "To be successful, do not pursue success, pursue competence", a half-truth which ignores integrity. 'Successful' is defined in terms of how much one makes in the profession. One professional counselor on enquiry about his present practice said, "Ahh! It is not good these days. Very few come for therapy after this mad Christian group started their assembly in town".

In the thick of all these apparently anti-Christian postures in every echelon of society, a genuinely committed Christian, called out to bless others through counseling, has to choose his path to get ahead and be of service to the needy in pain and suffering. Choosing a path is easier when compared to the going. You need a vehicle to get going and have to be careful to have a hold on your handle that you may direct the going and be spared of possible falling.

FOREWORD TO HEALING PRESENCE

I am extremely privileged and happy to write the forward to this great unique book written by Dr. Alex Mathew PhD. I consider it a fortune because what is described in this unique masterpiece is not an idea but a TRUTH, a REALITY and in fact LIFE itself.

My acquaintance with Dr. Alex Mathew goes back more than three decades and ever since I have known him, my life changed and took an about turn. I still remember an evening walk with him many years back, when I was sharing with him some of my concerns. As we were walking, he took a plant from the wayside and told me "Just like these branches abide in the plant, you should abide in Christ Jesus like a branch in the Vine." That truth statement started working in my life and I can never forget that evening and that quote from the Holy Word. It attracted me deep within the Love-Truth which IS that great I AM. It was again confirmed to me when I read from the great servant of the Most High E. Stanley Jones on the 'absolute dependence and perfect confidence we have in the Lord Jesus Christ'.

Over the years I have found that this great anointed servant of the Lord Dr. Alex Mathew (uncle, as I address him fondly) has been the instrument of this LOVE-TRUTH (Jesus Christ Himself) in moldings and mentoring innumerable lives across the globe, both young and old from all walks of life. I have learnt from him that abiding is not a philosophy but life itself. In fact, his own life of love, humility and ministering and mentoring is the absolute living testimony to the Meta-Love-Counseling which he portrays in this book. About 30 years back he had a heart surgery but that did not deter him from being fruitful for the Lord and investing in people's lives. Thanks to the Lord.

As he argues rightly, the Christian counselor must be able to differentiate between secular 'knowledge' and spiritual wisdom. He has contrasted the most popular counseling systems as practiced in our country with the true Meta-Love-counseling. In his own words "You love others because you experience the Love-Truth that is Christ and feel comfortably joyful in pouring it out for others. Your heart is constrained by the Love of Christ to reach out to those who are in all sorts of pain. This is not an easy task. It takes a lot of determination and disarming commitment to be doing such a godly service. The credibility of the Christian Meta-love- counselor is her/his identity in Christ, more than the academic qualifications. So be a counselor who abides in Jesus Christ as His branch."

Hence, this precious book reflects the author's deep understanding of His divine Master and a very deep walk with Him for many decades. It is a result of his varied real-life experiences and highly professional encounters too. He has his peculiar style of writing and it warrants a quiet, unprejudiced, and devotional reading to grasp the great practical truths portrayed here. It is a must read for all counselors and for all who want to have a deeper walk with the Lord in His service. I recommend this book highly to all to read it to the last word and get immersed in the LOVE-TRUTH Who IS and IS the Divine Eternal Truth which is ALL and in ALL.

Rev. Dr. Jacob K. Jacob
Bishop of Rapha Believers Church
Professor of Medicine
Bethel, Kalamassery, Ernakulam.

CONTENTS

1 Ordinary understanding of Christian Counseling..... 1

2 Available schools and systems of Counseling Therapies 7

3 Why I Want to be a Counselor 24

4 Freedom from 'dis' 'eases' 27

5 Emergence of Wisdom 31

6 Analysis / Counseling in a rush 39

7 Counseling vs Comfort fixing 50

8 Counseling used as a money-spinner 57

9 Counselor Qualities 62

10 Distortions 81

11 Know love and its varieties 89

12 Prayer and belonging 101

13 With gentleness 105

14 The path to blessings 112

15 Being Alert 116

16 Purpose and Priority 122

17 Need to define Chrstian Counseling 131

18 Meta-love-counseling is.......164
19 How does it work.......173
20 Dimensions of Meta-love-counseling.......190
21 Meta-love-counseling is operations of Love.......213
22 Taking lessons from counseling of Jesus.......222
23 Love in action, love makes it happen.......252
24 The basic tenets of Christian-
Meta -love -counseling.......271

PETAL-1

ORDINARY UNDERSTANDING OF CHRISTIAN COUNSELING

Counseling finds application in all areas of human existence like, relationships, anger, bitterness, calculations, desperation, depression, envy, fear, guilt, hatred, insecurity, jealousy, knavery, lethargy, meanness, nagging, obscenity, pains, quackery, remorse, suspicions, threats, unforgiveness, vindictiveness, worry, zealotry; to mention only one condition per alphabet.

What in the universe is any problem that is not created by man? (Except some natural calamities including genetic aberrations, epidemics and accidents) God finds all things He made are good. God girds us and holds and moves us and everything in the universe. Every form of energy is in His control, from the subatomic particles to the macro Electromagnetic, Gravity, the Strong Force and the Weak force. Everything in this universe responds to divine validation. That is the basic Indian ethos too.

Everything in this universe deserves love and He holds and guides all things in His Love. We have no mandate not to love. In other words we shall not hate, shall not be indifferent and shall be free from all minor forms of sinfulness. We are not to worship anything other than the Love-Truth, which made and maintained all things. Everything deserves love, because everything is worthy of love. I dare not say worthy of my love. Because love is not mine only to give as I may feel, but my being is in love, made of Love, and that makes all things are given to me with the express mandate to love. In making of all things, He invested love in all things including you and me.

Love is that which gives of itself. Love holds all things together, including you and me in His grasp. Love seeps into me and fills me to overflow.[5] My cup runneth over –Psalm. 23: 5) That I may pour out to others that which fills me. Specific manner of giving love may differ depending on the specific dispenser. The non-living are just there to give. What it gives of itself depends on what it is and what is taken off from it.

As for you and me, we are made in the image of the Maker. You are the same material as I am. Same image, same materials, yet appearance may differ, manifestations differ. All are made to be good, yet all do not turnout good, as all have fallen short of goodness invested in them. The 'fallen-ness' differs as it is allowed the freedom to grow or grunt or otherwise. What causes differences are the components or their combinations! The indwelling content and the nature of the container differ. Content contaminates the container or is it the other way round? It is a question worthy of asking for which I have no answer. Altered nature of the content or the container would be manifested. This is in tune with the angle and degree of alteration. Some get dented, some get distorted and destroyed. Some degenerate, some disintegrate on the way. Some turn fragrant, spreading sweet aroma. Some evolve lovely and spread love all the way. Some die within and emit stink polluting the inside and outside. Indwelling extra contents make all the difference, damaging the container too; we should assume.

Since all are of one and from one, each one belongs to everyone. This is the truth as best as we can hold. That is why that One says, love everyone as I love. Seen that way it is so simple to follow. So I need to love as Love-Truth loves me. I need to love without asking for love in return; without asking anything in return including any considerations of any kind. I must let it be known to myself that I need to love because I am loved. Not everyone else needs to know that I love anyone because; my love is not for just anyone but for everyone. Everyone needs to know I will not be without love, for they will know my love as their lives touch me.

Our charter to love is from Him who is Love-Truth. The charter is to receive and transport love, to all needy hearts and suffering lives, to all areas of deprivation and brokenness within our reach. He indicates our constituency; right where we are; where we have not cared to look, lay failed love and wasted lives. Our commission is to go to the ends of the earth. The earth lies all around us and we stand right in its center. All around us is pain obvious in all its hues and we pretend we do not see. That is not our problem we tend to think. We see pain all around but we find nothing to share. Pain is made livable in sharing love to the paining. The unshared love accumulates and rots in its choking piles like unused butter turning rancid. The rancid love piles within us polluting us from within. We come out turning the same into fuming anger. We may not appear as dragons. But from our tongues spread piercing flames. Flames hardly have the soothing touch which the broken lives crave. What do we gain withholding our love and seethe in fire instead? This is not just our individual problem only.

We have a guarantee that we can have His love. That is a conditional provision; His love will fill us, if we abide in his love. Then it follows that we need to come to live in his Words too. The sequence is, abide in His Word; in Him and ask to get all needs met. There would then be much beyond the asking to receive. His fruits produced in us, in His time for all to share and our lives become worthwhile; specifically fulfilling our commission. You have chosen to be a teacher or perhaps an IT professional, or a truck driver or a money maker or homemaker; perhaps to be a plumber, a mason or a carpenter or a painter. It may be in advertising or in acting, shoe polishing or peanut vending. Does not matter what one does. What is the purpose behind all doings? There is space for doing the good and spreading love everywhere in every profession. This possibility exists along with space to hurt others. In the same space dwell these inseparable twin forces of love and indifference. They fight within for greater expression of each. None of these will be expressed unless you allow it. The power of choice and expression of either is with you, within you. The fight within is normal and usual, perhaps inevitable; it is here and now you realize your great strength to choose. Take a look within, taking real time looking at everything; all that has invaded your inside and its doings. What is the picture you get? Reflect that picture on to the backdrop of your heart. A loving Christian Meta-love- counselor sees the shining image of love that makes all things possible for the good of others. This is where you get the initiation to act in love.

There are other ways you may choose to look, or you may not care to take a look at all. That is a preferred choice of yours. Or you may choose to ignore what you see. And let Love and indifference coexist within you, bisecting you. Love and hate are bedfellows within, feuding for expression. At the proximal end of expression, it is your choice. That is the point that makes the vital shifts in life. All that comes out of you is a matter of your choice and initiation. The choice depends on who reigns in your life. Love-Truth within you talks one language you know. The language spoken by evil too is familiar to you. You know better where your expertise lies; the strange bedfellows compete to offer you help. Wisdom in Scripture says you cannot serve two masters. Together these two masters will take away any peace you want to keep. Wisdom will confer; one of them has to go. You have to gather courage to kill that part which blends with bad and provokes evil. Once free from choking evil, the rest of you is redeemed. The redeemed reflect the new. In the redeemed resides the new. Paul said,[6] "I am crucified with Christ, I no longer live". That 'I'; was the bad self that controlled Saul that was to be Paul. If I too let that 'I' control me I am dead in my 'self'. The dead self in me will only be good enough to stink; spreading poison and polluting the very environs I am part of. "Christ lives in me" makes all the difference in making me new.

From now on the new 'me' has to be the vehicle to take love to the ends of the earth. To me then comes the commission,[7] Mat.28:: 19- 200 "Go therefore and make disciples of all the nations, baptizing them in the name of the Father and the Son and the Holy Spirit teaching them all that I have commanded you; and lo, I am with you always, even to the end of the age" NASB. The love that makes me new, love that fills me, constrains me to be on the go; being and doing good.

What means I choose to spread that love that fills me, is again my preferred choice. I personally was entrusted with counseling which evolved into Meta-love counseling or a Healing Presence. What is your choice? You have all the freedom as befits your person. Be on the go; that is all that matters. Get back to the base principles everyday and be on the road. You cannot sit idle when love constrains you to love, to serve, to respect, to cherish, to witness and to build others up. Love moves you and me to be on the go. I know you are on your way. I know you are with me. I also know that the Lord is with us in this journey – to counsel in his name and on His behalf. Praise His holy name.

PETAL-2

AVAILABLE SCHOOLS AND SYSTEMS OF COUNSELING THERAPIES

Having said all that we said in the earlier chapter, let us take a brief look at the different systems that go around in the name of counseling.

Analytical, Behavioral, Classical Psychoanalysis, Cognitive, Constructional, Cross-cultural, Eclectic, Faith, Humanistic, Hypnotic, Neuro-linguistic Programming Religious, Sham, Superstition, Systemic;

And its sections and subsections of all these schools; for example

Collective unconscious of Carl Jung,

Individual psychotherapy of Alfred Adler;

Client Centered Therapy of Carl Rogers,

Peak Experience of Abraham Maslow,

Object Relations of Erik Erikson,

Mutualist- self-therapy of Joseph de Rivera and then

Play therapy, Gestalt, Group Therapy, Implosive therapy,

Cognitive therapies of Albert Ellis/Aaron Beck

Search for meaning of Viktor Frankle

Richard Bandler and John Grinder with Neuro-linguistic programming

Family Therapy, Feminist Therapy, Group Therapy, Re-evaluation therapy, Reality Therapy, and a whole lot of therapies numbering close to over a thousand or more in the market as of now.

We can compile a long list of Therapists including, Karen Horney, Erich Fromm, Gordon Allport, Thomas Harris, and the redoubtable comfort vendors like Sadguru, besides Eckhart Tolle. Mehta and Khare and a hoard of life-skill Master orators and their kin too need to be recognized in collective groups reaching in this area.

Let us try to make a large inclusive definition of Counseling as we ordinarily understand it

Ordinarily counseling can be said to be for the purpose of empathetically helping, teaching, advising, leading, informing, guiding, enabling, walking along, relating empathetically, goading and causing changes, admonishing gently, at times urging, by and large reaching professional help to those in need of wellbeing. Granted that most all counseling interactions remain confidential, non-judgmental, and in unconditional acceptance with positive regard; the sharing, modifying of views, experiences, attitudes and behavior are the main usable tools. The individual in need is given a new perspective on the present situation to gain more clarity towards achieving desired goals. Counseling is expected to elicit from the paining person what lies at the root of the issues that cloud the vision of that person and give clear directions to navigate through life's challenges. Individuals and families searching for resolution of their problems are empowered to identify and resolve their concerns, easing their stress levels to find relief. A certain degree of gentle unobvious marginally innocuous manipulations are inbuilt in all these systems; all the same qualified as manipulations.

We need to be conscious of the fact that in every human interaction there is an element of counseling for the good or bad depending on the individual's goals and instances involved. This happens even without the parties involved ever sensing that something is happening and causing changes in their views of their present and possible future situations. Any counselor with a private hidden agenda can wreck havocs in any type of counseling interactions.

All types of counseling make use of its own private tools and techniques to comfortably guide the needy individuals through difficult problems in feelings, thoughts, behavior in internal and external expressive patterns. Despite the differences in the schools of counseling the essential operations of counseling are client-centered through person-to-person verbal interactions often inadvertently or not turning into investigative methods. Counselors gain some insights into the problems of the clients through other intuitive means depending on the training and experience that a counselor may possess. But; whatever the school of counseling, whatever system followed, whatever methods employed, whichever therapies prescribed and dispensed, whatever methodologies instituted, whatever enhancing goals set, whichever decision making promoted, whatever analytical scrutiny organized, whichever investigational tools employed, whatever interventional means resorted, whichever fraying relationships reshaped, whichever depressive tendencies uplifted, whatever seething anger cooled down, whatever violence pacified, whatever unforgiveness forsaken, whatever guilt remitted, whatever shame overthrown, whatever fear dislodged, whichever generalized angst neutralized; counseling remains largely a helping tool for those in various needs, hoping for a release from their particular trials.

In the next chapter itself, we shall take a very brief look into the constructs of some of the more touted and popular varieties of counseling making its round in the society. Some of the more widely known Schools of counseling alphabetically arranged are given below.

Analytical, Behavioral, Classical Psychoanalysis, Cognitive, Constructional, Cross-cultural Eclectic, Faith, Humanistic, Hypnotic, Programming, Religious, Sham, Superstition, Systemic; as we already mentioned, all these techniques amounting to more than roughly near a thousand are for bringing in positive improvement in the clients' life. The ultimate intended purpose of any counseling ought to be restoration of the wholeness in the seeker of wellbeing; the client or the counselee. It is not practical here, to go into an elaborate descriptive detailing of the various types of counseling tenets that do its round in the society. Let us take in brief the examples of a couple of very popular and widely practiced varieties practiced in this country.

i. Neuro-Linguistic Programming. ii) Rogarian; Client-centered therapy and iii) Transactional Analysis.

NEURO-LINGUISTIC PROGRAMING

There are 'n' number of therapies with tall claims and promises of instant and total relief from all problems. At the moment NLP is one of the widely touted Schools. A closer observation of these panaceas would tell us some are classic business practices. I propose to place before you some unaltered research findings for you to go through and arrive at your own conclusions. Some of the popular techniques that are being popularized in the market would make you cry, especially when you see it is largely practiced by those who call themselves 'Christians' in deliberately louder voices.

Let us first take the case of Neuro-Linguistic-Programming. NLP may be thought of as a system of Psychology concerned with self-development of the human being through studying of subjective experiences and programming people through fabricated techniques.

Techniques in NLP include:-

Rapport, Anchoring, Swish, Reframing, Six steps reframe, Ecology, Congruency and Parts integration; all esoteric terms!

"A basic assumption of NLP is that internal mental processes such as problem solving, memory, and language consists of visual auditory, kinesthetic (and possibly olfactory and gustatory) representations that are engaged when people think about problems, task or activities or engage in them"[8] Enhancing Human Performance: Issus, Theories, and Techniques. (Drukman and Swets (Eds); National Academy Press, 1988).

You be the judge of what constancy an assumption of the assuming person would have on a multifactor representation of people thinking about problems both of which are totally subjective mental transactions.

NLP techniques generally aim to change behavior through modifying internal representations, examining the way a person represents a problem and by building desirable representations of alternative outcomes or goals. In addition, Bandler and Grinder claimed that the representational system used could be tracked using eye movements, gestures, breathing, sensory predicates and other cues in order to improve rapport and social influence"[9]. (Bandler, R., Grinder. J, Frogs into Princes: Neuro Linguistic Programming. Real Peoples Press: 1979).

> In simpler terms it is telling you, if you may let yourself be Programmed you can turn yourself from the frog you are to the prince you are destined to be. Who will hesitate to buy that sort of a packet?

[10]Christopher F. Sharpley in 1984 found "little research evidence is supporting its usefulness as an effective counseling tool" about NLP in the Journal of Counseling Psychology, 1987, Vol.34. But technicians would muse; "That is no problem as long as we can convince as many as we can and collect fat fees".

> [11]"Certainly research data do not support the rather extreme claims that proponents of NLP have made as to the validity of its principles or the novelty of its procedures" (Sharpley C.F.) "Research findings on Neuro-linguistic Programming: Non supportive Data or An Untestable Theory. Communication and Cognition" (Journal of Counseling Psychology'.1987, Vol.34, No.1). Yet there are eager technicians, predominantly in 'Christian communities' vending this overtly misleading rip-off. Sharpley further states that "NLP may be seen

as a partial compendium of rather than as an original contribution to counseling practice and, thereby, has a value distinct from the lack of research data supporting the underlying principle that Bandler and Grinder posited to present NLP as a new magical theory". He goes on to say, "as a counseling tool, the techniques and underlying theory unique to NLP, were both empirically invalidated and unsupported but that if NLP is presented as a theory-less set of procedures gathered from many approaches to counseling, then it may serve as a reference role for therapist who wish to supplement their counseling practice by what may be novel techniques to them".

The idea that we get from this well written and researched article is that NLP serves as a money making tool for therapists looking out for magical and impressionable techniques to dupe people looking for healing therapies.

The psychological techniques study committee directed by,[12] Druckman "found little if any evidence to support NLP's assumptions or that it is effective as a strategy for social influence". (Neuro Linguistic Programming, From Wikipedia, http://en.wikipedia.org/wiki/Neuro-linguistic-Programing).

"......original interest in NLP turned to disillusionment over the research and now it is rarely even mentioned in Psychotherapy"[13] (Efran, J.S. Lukens M.D. Language, structure, and change: frameworks of meaning in psychotherapy; W. W. Norton NY p.122, 1990).

Yet there are people paying up to Rs.5, 000 for 3-day workshop sessions of NLP in our country and high profile technicians who get away with it. "NLP is a thoroughly fake title designed to give the impression of scientific respectability" (Coraballis. M C).[14] "Are we in our right minds" Sala, S. (Ed).

[15]Mind Myths: Exploring Assumptions about Mind and Brain. Wiley, John Sampsons, 1999 (pp. 25-41).

Thetruthisweareoutofourmindsascribingcredibility to such duping.[16] "In the late 1980s Sharpley's (1984, 1987) research reviews in experimental counseling psychology and by the United States National Research Council gave NLP an overall negative assessment marking a decrease in NLP research interest". (Wikipedia – http://en.wikipedia.org/wiki/Neuro-linguistic-Programing).

What is said in the above quotes from the works of highly respected research scholars is straightforward proof of the futility of pursuing a therapy like NLP.

Promoting such systems only indicates the sick state of comfort-vending that goes on in the name of Programming and fixing people. Such systems flourish because there are people who do not know these systems for what they are and unwittingly buy these, trusting in its effectiveness. As a Christian counselor you have the responsibility to warn and save suggestible dewy-eyed aspirants of comfort from drinking from the broken cisterns of the secular arid zones.

Are these looters doing it out of love and are for the glossy-eyed consumers? The un-exhibited quality in all is to exploit the gullible and the fickle minded weak, to line their pockets[17]. That is [NLP] Neuro-Linguistic Programming for you, if you care to know. It will also open your eyes to know that NLP was developed as an advertising tool sadly and craftily turned into a counseling Tool. *('Making of a Christian Counselor';. Alex Mathew, Authentic books -2008)*

ii. Rogarian, client-centered counseling.

Client centered or person to person counseling is in wider use around. Over the years, most practitioners in their own time shift to eclectic or combination practices. There are as many counseling patterns as there are a number of practitioners. This is inevitable as individual styles differ and what is convenient for each, creeps into individual practices.

The nine steps of the Rogarian model can be better put across in a tabular form. :------

PRE – HELPING PHASE				
	STAGE - 1	STAGE - 2	STAGE – 3	STAGE - 4
	ACQUAINTING	**OBSERVING**	**FOUNDING**	**DIAGNOSING**
COUNSELOR'S SKILL	Rapport Building Familiarizing 1. Welcoming 2. Providing Privacy 3. Small talk 4. Confidentiality 5. Time – limit 6. Previous Counseling 7. Invitation to talk	Looks for cues to understanding the non-verbal behavior of the counselee 1. Non-verbal behavior (Body language) 2. Energy level 3. Eye movements, Hand & Arm gestures, Arm & Leg, Barriers, Head gestures etc.	▫ Attends, Listens and responds ▫ Reflects the content ▫ Reflects the Feeling ▫ Reflects the deeper feeling (Total Attending)	Finds out if the counselee suffers from 1. Faulty Situation 2. Faulty Thinking 3. Faulty Feeling 4. Faulty Behaviour Pinpoints the problem, asks for a recent event.

	ASSOCIATING	MANIFESTING	INVOLVING	INVESTIGATING
COUNSELLE'S TASK	Accepts and co-operates with the initiatives of the counselor by associating with him 1. Willingness 2. Creates Responsibility 3. Fear of change 4. Reluctant Counselee 5. Resistant Counselee 6. Silences	Continues to cooperate with the counselor, maintaining at least a workable relationship	Gets involved and starts expressing	Investigates what has gone wrong with her/him

POST – HELPING PHASE				
STAGE – 5	STAGE – 6	STAGE – 7	STAGE – 8	STAGE – 9
Stage -5 **PACING**	**Stage -6** **PERSONALIZING**	**Stage -7** **REFRAMING**	**Stage-8** **INITIATING**	**Stage- 9** **EVALUATING**
Responds to the counselee's internal frame of reference with the attitudes 1. Genuineness 2. Respect 3. Basic Empathy 4. Concreteness	▫ Integrative understanding ▫ Personalizes the counselee's deficiencies Personalizes 1. Meaning 2. Problem 3. Goal	▫ Stimulating the counselee to have an alternative frame of reference with the attitudes. 1. Alternative frame of Reference 2. Advanced empathy 3. Challenging 4. Self-disclosure 5. Immediacy	▫ Initiates – Problem solving techniques, behavioral strategies, and action programs by setting goals and making contracts	▫ Checks how the client has fared ▫ Gets a feedback as to how the client has fared with her/his decisions and if need modifies the means and goals
EXPLORING	**UNDERSTANDING**	**REORIENTING**	**ACTING**	**REVIEWING**
Engages herself/himself with deep exploring	Dynamically self understands by owning her/his contribution to the problem	Develops alternative and constructive ways of thinking, feeling and behaving	Appropriates the desired change by taking appropriate steps	Reviews the steps taken; modifies if necessary; fulfills her/his contracts

All these nine stages are activities designed to goad the counselee into action are nothing short of gentle manipulations yet infinitely better than other commercial modes. My position is that the counselor has no right to manipulate a counselee at any stage whatever, in any system of counseling. That is the subject matter in 'Healing Presence' or what we designate as 'Meta-love-counseling'.

iii. Transactional Analysis or TA

TA is a popular psychological analysis based on the concept that individual behavior patterns and social relationships reflect an interchange between parental, adult and childlike aspects of personal angularities developing from early life experiences.

Transactional analysis was introduced in the psychoanalytical scene in the 1950s and it was a widely practiced counseling methodology till late the 70s. From then on it became unpopular and now practically no one serious about analysis in counseling will touch it even with a ten foot pole.

As counseling fascinates people, schools like Transactional Analysis gained popularity because of the ease with which it can be practiced. No wonder eager aspirants fired up by blind enthusiasm, flock to learn these redoubtable methods to gain some footing in this discipline for reasons that surface as in the section below.

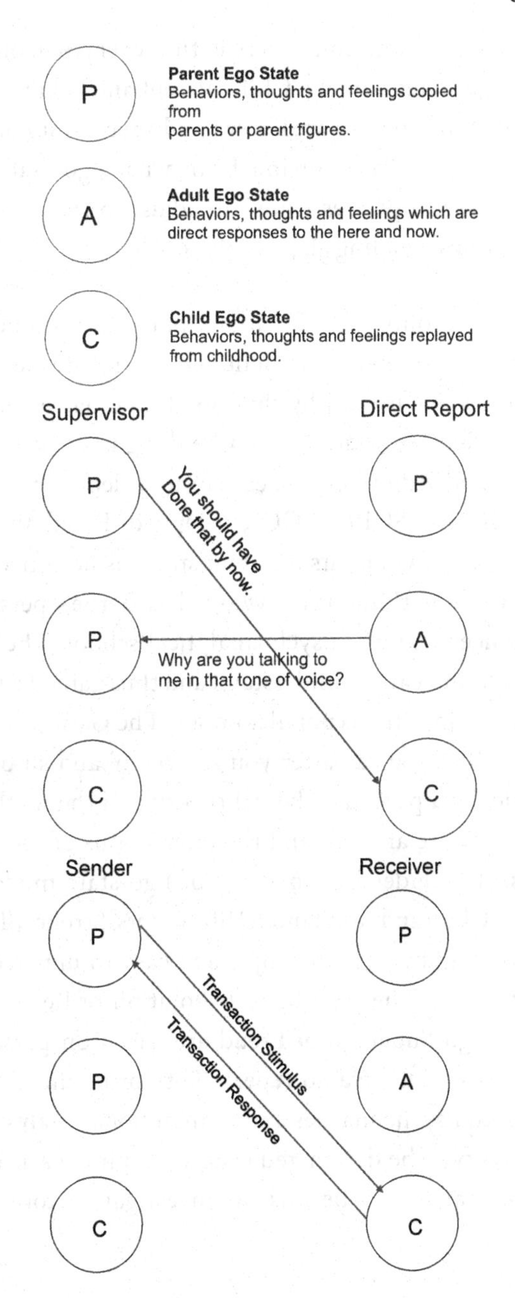
P
Parent Ego State
Behaviors, thoughts and feelings copied from
parents or parent figures.
A
Adult Ego State
Behaviors, thoughts and feelings which are direct responses to the here and now.
C
Child Ego State
Behaviors, thoughts and feelings replayed from childhood.
Supervisor
Direct Report
P
P
You should have Done that by now.
P
A
Why are you talking to me in that tone of voice?
C
C
Sender
Receiver
P
P
Transaction Stimulus
Transaction Response
P
A
C
C

The basic assumption of TA is that every person has three ego states namely; Child, Parent and Adult. If the ego-states of a person are known and anyone interacting with that person, knowing from what ego state the other person operates from can adjust to the personal interactions avoiding all possible conflicts.

TA is not only Post-Freudian but extra Freudian, according to its proponent Dr. Eric Berne. TA maintains that unhealthy childhood experiences lead to pathological ego-states, which he designated as Child, Parent and Adult ego states. He took leave from the ID, EGO and SUPEREGO concepts of Freud and got tackled to EGO and its different states as he conceived it. The whole thing has developed as Berne's personal differences with the Psychoanalytical school. The idea is simple and easy to understand and thus gained a wide followership with his popular books 'The Games People Play' 'What you say after you say, hello' and so on. It is basically a psychoanalytical theory and the methods of therapy are analysis and the interactions of the ego-states. It includes the concepts of Ego-state model of Parent, Child and Adult model life Scripts, Strokes, Time structure and....It is so simple and easy to understand and practice. The ego-states elaboration of Berne and the Id, Ego Superego of Freud are based on personal opinions which have no repeatability or predictability, thus both Psychoanalysis and Transactional analysis do not qualify to be designated even as empirical sciences. Psychoanalysis, at best is an investigative tool and

Transactional analysis is investigative plus a comfort balm massage therapy.

Much need not be said about this very popular therapy even in the 2020s other than the results it produced for Dr. Berne himself[18]. Dr. Berne married three times. His second wife died. At the time of his funeral both the surviving wives did not attend the funeral. (Wikipedia) That suffices to say about the effectiveness of this mode of therapy.

PETAL-3

WHY I WANT TO BE A COUNSELOR

During my over fifty years of counseling I have trained thousands of people in counseling and in nearly all courses I have given out a questionnaire asking them 'Why do I want to be a Counselor'. Below is the sample of the questionnaire with some marginal changes and responses evaluated. You can use the same for self-evaluation.

This central and crucial fact should be clearly and unambiguously understood by all who aspire to be counselors.

(Please tick any three options which are closer to your personal preference)

1. I like to help people
2. I think it is a respectable profession.
3. I want to show people the right choices in life
4. My Church and my people expect me to be in a helping profession.

5. I have an MSW and Counseling as a special paper and I believe I can be a good counselor
6. Something within me tells to take up counseling
7. The Love of Christ constrains me
8. I want to learn how to adjust to my life circumstances.
9. I want to create a good relationships within my own family
10. I see, there is good demand for counselors in Education institutions
11. I think I can bring peace within a fighting family
12. There is personal joy in bringing people together in oneness.
13. I am sick of the way people unthinkingly get into fighting and react to violent acts
14. For sharing the comfort I receive from God and with others around me
15. I get acceptance as a counselor and honor in society.
16. I can start this as a profession with minimum investment
17. I do not have to go hunting for a job when I can earn a living, being a counselor.
18. I am in HR and counseling is an important part of my profession.
19. I want to put right the dislocations in relationships within my own family.
20. My own life will be better off with some training in Counseling
21. What is the whole purpose of my life with so much suffering around me?

22. I am doing a University program in Psychology and I want to specialize in counseling.

    (If you are planning to take this test, please do not continue to read below this)

    There are twenty-two statements and nineteen of them are self centered answers not totally valid for opting counseling as a profession. Of the five hundred randomly selected answer sheets, there were only 17 responses which selected all the three right answers.

None of the nineteen answers are irrelevant. All have some useful and meaningful aspects to it. But 'I' and 'me' are at the core of all the nineteen answers. I did not nor do I disapprove of the answers, because all said and done; when a person chooses a career possibility, it is inevitable that everyone looks for the possible benefits and profits therein. The expected right choices are 7, 14 and 21 in which the scholar's motive is to go beyond self and be of some blessing to others. Ideally all sorts of counseling ought to be for the express benefit of the person seeking your help. As you would see stated elsewhere in this book; ordinarily counseling can be said to be for the purpose of pointedly helping, teaching, advising, leading, guiding, enabling, walking along, relating empathetically, goading and causing changes, admonishing gently, at times urging, by and large reaching professional help to those in need of wellbeing. In all manner of counseling, these traditional functions do happen in limited or larger dimensions.

PETAL-4

FREEDOM FROM 'DIS' 'EASES'

Are you game for a surprise?

> Apart from accidents, infectious diseases and natural calamities more than 85 percent of our problems are caused by us!
>
> This is not a surprise!
>
> We are more or less helpless where viruses, bacteria, protozoan, fungal pathogens and faulty lifestyles bring on sicknesses. Whatever the source of sicknesses, it is mostly preceded by varieties of pain, fever, diarrhea, fatigue, muscle aches, weight loss, and so on.

In sickness we feel bad, ailing, down, ill, indisposed, peaky, cruddy, lousy, sickish, troubled and poorly. Besides, we feel fed up, angry, displeased, at times enraged, horn-mad, indignant, almost furious and outraged, irate, livid, simply upset and worked up, complicating our sick condition. It takes away our sense of wellbeing or ease and so we call it a disease. In fact, it is 'dis'-'ease'!

What is mentioned above in the paragraph are all feelings; in other words emotions. Are we honest enough to say that we are responsible for not taking hold of our emotions? In a later chapter we will have a detailed look at the wholeness of human beings and see that feelings triggered by emotions are part of what we understand as the 'Mind'. What is mind? Where is the mind? Some would say it is the brain; in the head, some vaguely say it is in the heart. Thousands of simultaneous reactions occur in every cell or organelle causing shifts in the electromagnetic field. Every experience is felt by all cells at the same time. Reactions within a cell send out messages across the cell membrane in and out all the time. An emotion may raise the energy level and particle interaction locally and all over the body. The whole integrated organism functions as the mind. The actions of the peptides in the neural network do not stand alone; all the cell activities are coordinated in the integrated whole being. Does it come as a surprise?

He, who knows Love, knows how to lovingly respond to life. Those who exist in the subjective, searching and analytical mode of existence are more often incapable of responding in love as they have a personal agenda for gain in one form or another. They are likely to react in evident manners or suppress the reaction within causing further suffering. Reactions are not preceded by thoughts but kicked up by instinctive drives for instant gratification. Reactions are always in anger; but responses invariably are in peaceable love. Consequences in the two types of interactions are only easily imaginable.

Anger is not a comfortable answer for any situation in life whereas a loving response is the sign of maturity and godliness. Emotionally driven lives cannot be open for the revealing truth, vital in the imminent moment.

The ability to respond in love is the mark of personal growth. Capacity to knowingly turn away from anger goes side by side with such maturing growth. When progressive growth remains stunted, regression in some form or the other necessarily occurs. 'An idle mind is the workshop of the devil' is a sensible adage. This workshop gets cluttered with all sorts of negative thoughts triggering irritation to begin with, which gradually develop into resentment and brooding. Brooding hatches up ways to get even with the offending adversary; real or imagined. Pondering over the injustice inherent in the situation you prepare to execute your plans and may get into altercations, violent rebuttals or even acts of violence. No good thoughts about others have a place in a calculating mind. As you work up your mind to hateful rebuttals, and your body into appropriate hurting action or non-action; all the time your inner burden keeps increasing. Let-down anger, failure, hatred, unforgiveness and guilt are normal byproducts in this work-up.

All the thoughts are on getting even or on possible failure to get there. End result is increased burden in the brain and the total organism come under stress and inclusive loss of ease which we call 'dis' ease. If nothing is done to reduce the stress, the brain and the body take alternate paths to gain balance which result in further perplexing, the 'dis' ease. Ignoring the manipulations of the cluttered mind is always an injurious game. All sorts of contorted schemes take shape within the individual pushing him further into serious confused states of dis 'ease', crying for action. Dis 'eases' are caused by our interpretation of events that happen around us, through things that we hear from people whose opinions we value and our ardent efforts to offset the effects of pains caused by such happenings. The absence of appreciation of our goodness from people whom we care too can hurt. We cannot help the hurts caused by other people. It is within their right to say or do things which please them. All people have the right to do or say what they what they want done or otherwise. It is not our province to correct them but to take care that such hurting words or acts do not cause cluttering of our thoughts and inflict wounds in our minds, by which I mean our whole being. When we do that we are actually buying their problems and making it ours.

For ease and peace of our minds, we need to un-clutter our inner world. We have a serious mandate to forgive others. Without a forgiving conduct of a serene lifestyle in resurrected newness; power for good is impossible. Forgiveness frees you from the need for manipulation and calculations, freeing you from slavery to vengeful thoughts. That gives real freedom from dis 'ease'. Is that also a surprise?

PETAL-5

EMERGENCE OF WISDOM

Christian counselor must be deeply aware of the mysterious story of how she/he was claimed, redeemed, and invited into a life in an abiding relationship with the Holy One. It means interiorized awareness of the content of the abiding relationship. The process of the change of heart accompanying abiding and the impact it has on the personal makeup of the counselor is to be profitably passed on to the people in need as she/he once stood.

In Christian counseling, the counselor cannot afford to place undue eminence on logic, rational thinking, and empirical evidence leading to pure knowledge. Knowledge by itself is capable of producing a Frankenstein of a counselor. In Christian-meta-love- counseling there is a need for intuitive responses based on resources beyond knowledge. The singular Christian resource is revelation without which a counselor would succeed in fixing people in need, but not blessing. Blessing is bound to be beyond sheer words and pure knowledge employing rhetoric.

Knowledge – Emotions

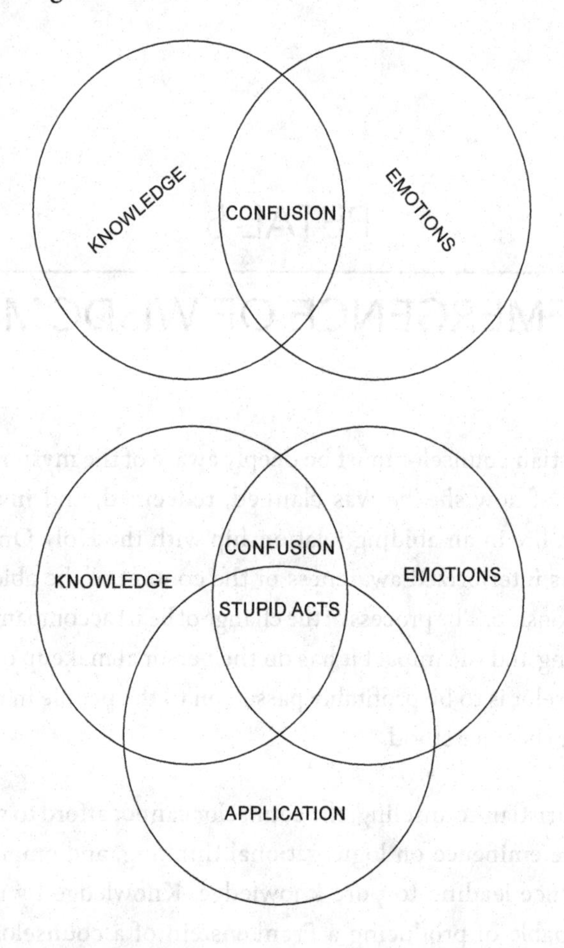

The Christian counselor should be a person capable of rightly interpreting life experiences. Knowledge without a belief system would tend to interpret life from an emotional base. In the interaction of knowledge and emotion, only confusion and conflicts arise. Where faith seasons knowledge, wisdom emerges.

Faith by itself, however, will only help to produce religious fanatics who could turn into terrorists dreaming salvation through killing those who believe anything in different frames. The ilk of such is not rare.

Interpreting life from the interface of knowledge and faith, a person comes out with his best. I am trying to point out the need to look at life and live life with a sturdy faith base in order to be able to provide the best of services to those we hope to bless.

Knowledge – Faith based Value system

The Christian counselor must be able to differentiate between secular 'knowledge' and spiritual wisdom. A highly 'educated' person may not be wise in terms of important life issues. A British Prime Minister (Arthur Wellesley, 1828) remarked, 'Educate people without religion and you make them clever devils'. He may have said that vexed by political chicanery. I do not want to say upsetting things about the counseling or political scenes, but I will not be far from the facts that our education system is bending backwards to produce very clever devils with whom I once was in league.

It is also important to keep in mind that the gross and subjective perceptions would limit a Christian counselor, hindering his/her progress to become a fully Christian person. Mentioning this may seem a bit out of place here, but we need to realize that heart qualities differ from person to person. Those of us who think we have a perfect hold on our salvation experience and quite an assured abiding status, at times, may resort to our own preferred ways of thinking.

Such thinking and subsequent subjective acts may cause unusual and devastating upsets in the lives of those to whom we minister.

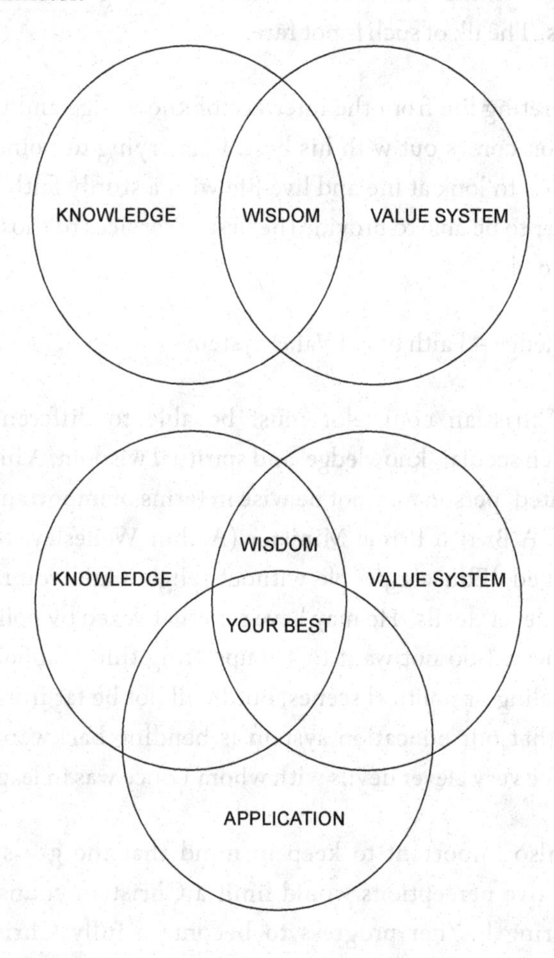

The Slides are self-speaking. Only from wisdom there is a chance for your BEST to emerge

The meta-love-counselor needs to be a co-traveler with the person in pain. She/he is not primarily an answer giver, but a calm, relaxed companion who meaningfully responds in tune with the whispering of the Holy Spirit to the person on pilgrimage to self-discovery. The person in need is likely to be in a vulnerable emotional state. Counseling provides for intimate sharing of painful details of personal life where the seductive possibilities are enormous. Discrete distancing from the hidden needs, passions and drives of the person in need and of the counselor herself/himself has to be in the foreground and in a clear field of vision for the meta-love-counselor. Take this as a major warning for many a stalwart has fallen in ugly, damp heaps to regret bitterly.

One point we have not touched in depth is the honesty of the meta-love-counselor. She/he needs to ask herself/himself this question, 'Can I be sure that I will always tell the truth in love? Will my Master and Lord give me license to lie? We all have a tendency to shuffle around with euphemistic platitudes fearing further hurt to the already paining person. We can with ease take the paining person on a theological expedition and make light of the pain. The counselor would do well to remember that it is truth which sets a person free (John 8:32). The Truth personified is waiting to bless the person.

Sharing the TRUTH and its imminent proximity from honest personal experience need not be a tightrope walk. Be refreshingly sincere in presenting the truth as you know, as you experience and as you would live it.

A further warning is relevant here. The counselor may risk the danger of assuming the IP, if not the VIP, role in the counseling transactions. In the guise of presenting the TRUTH, one may start broadcasting one's own virtues, perhaps unwittingly. A meta-love-counselor should be wary of this ever-present trap. The meta-love-counselor who allows himself to grow would be happy to be a basin and towel-bearing servant.

The meta-love-counselor along with the Holy Spirit is primarily with the counselee to listen to the groaning of that person in pain. Nothing should proceed from the counselor that would obstruct the flow of the Spirit and the receiving of it by the counselee. Jesus and His Spirit are waiting to bless this person. Everything that goes on in the counseling environment should be only that which facilitates the free flow of Spirit in the grace of the Lord Jesus.

The meta-love- counselor should be adept in not getting in the way of the healing that is the province of the Holy Spirit. I mean the meta-love-counselor should be sufficiently relaxed to allow the Holy Spirit to transact the business of disbursing the blessing without the impetuous meddling in eager enterprise. One does not have to play the CEO in a counseling situation. That will be an assumption of a nasty order, not becoming a Christian. I am not suggesting indifference and inactivity rather active waiting in assured expectancy of the working of the Omniactive Spirit.

Finally, all things that a Christian meta-love-counselor does ought to have a firm bearing on the Scripture. All counseling should emanate from that baseline. For the choice of right principles and right decisions and right application, the Christian meta-love-counselor must turn to the Bible and nothing else. This might upset a liberal Christian with secular leanings for whom every moral teaching is good enough for salvation. I was asked by many well meaning friends and fellow workers 'Why Christ only, why Bible only? There are so many good people following so many good teachings'. I do not have to be apologetic about the answer, as I have made the answer explicit elsewhere. I have no problem with any answer anyone may offer. For me the answer constitutes that fact that Christ is Truth, the Way and Life and the Bible is all about that Truth; the Way and Life.

The Bible is God's authoritative guide to make us competent in the ministry of counseling. We live in times where the Bible is attracting bad press. In the rush of secularism, derogating the Bible is a pet fashion of the so-called intelligentsia. Postmodernism has the run of the day, which maintains that all claims to truths are relative and there all truths deserve equal recognition. A Christian counselor, who contributes to postmodernism, even if unintentionally, would be willing for compromises, ready to use any system of counseling as valid. In order to appear justified he/she may garnish any particular type of counseling with shrewdly inserted Bible verses and call the whole thing as Christian. God forbid!

I have known a counselor with a high Christian profile. He wears on his neck a good sized wooden cross and displays big posters of Christ healing the blind man and the leper in his counseling office. He has an outsized Bible on his table. He declared he is eclectic. His main methods of counseling are Transactional Analysis (TA), Hypnotism, Panic Healing and Yoga. A good many of the clientele think he is a practicing Christian. The Bible plus questionable therapies declares our decaying faith structure. That does not honor God nor bless His people despite the market for soothing balms.

There are some who say rather loudly 'I am a vegetarian; I only eat chicken and fish'. That is fine. He has the freedom to do that. However, I doubt whether we can draw a parallel with someone saying, 'I am a Christian counselor; I only practice Transactional Analysis and Hypnotism'. It is rather tricky and not a wise idea navigating with feet in two different boats. When the tear does come finally, the resulting sight is bound to be ghastly.

PETAL-6

ANALYSIS / COUNSELING IN A RUSH

Christian counselors, teachers, intellectuals, scholars, research fellows, chatterboxes, hotheads and all who think their brain is their strength tend to use more of their 'intellect' and have an urge to correct others. They think they are recognized as more knowledgeable. They consider themselves experts equipped to correct others who are likely to be in the wrong according to them. As a rule they are good people with good intentions and at the ready to part with their advanced expert knowledge and richer experience. On scrutiny the experts find people make a mess of their lives by faulty coping mechanisms and wrong reactions to troubling incidents and individuals. They gather evidence of how people act in subjective compulsions basing their inferences on past experiences and thus precipitating problems for themselves. People lack the perseverance to take objective looks at their acts and non-acts thereby intensifying their anxiety and anguish; experts chant on. Quick ready-made remedies are available in these days of advanced motivational talks and life-style guides steeped in tech. Oh, what a relief! We have answers for all problems and if not we have very advanced medication with least side-effects and of course technological expertise.

Since they think they know how people get into tight and tough situations they consider it their duty to offer help. It is easy to notice how people react and how their past influences them. They only need insight and the willingness to take responsibility for their situations. It is so simple. "Here, let me help you". That is the right thing to do too by any human standard. Experts and specialists including counselors have a sense of urgency to produce results. Thoughtful analysis of all the factors involved and efficient and quick diagnosis are important in such moves.

We have no disagreement over the position that organic dislocations in cognition, comprehension and application due to shift in status of Neuro-chemicals need to be addressed on that level and treated as any other physical illnesses. When it comes to matters of the 'heart', as it were, dealing with anxious thoughts, fear, guilt, unforgiveness, lust, shame, shyness and the like, the matter takes a different turn. Subjective urge to gather evidence or objective drive to calculate and analyze do not produce any positive blessing in a rush. One has to grow beyond these ordinary human efforts and be connected to the divine assurance where all things are possible for those who believe in the impossible happening.

What happens in analysis? Let us look at a simple example from the study of a flower. As a student of Botany, I have done practical studies of knowing everything about a flower.

First, we lay the flower on the dissection tray. Observe the flower, enjoy the beauty of the specimen and make a diagram of the whole flower and label the parts. Then take out each part starting with the outer floral whorls; the calyx, draw each sepal, record its shape, aestivation etc, then each petal its shape, special shapes if any and its aestivation, androecia, each anther, its attachment, individual pollen; Gynoecia, the nature of the carpals, how ovule are attached in each ovary and so on and on till we label each part and get a total and thorough understanding of the flower.

At the end of it all, where is the flower? There is nothing more of the flower! Only its mangled debris remains! For a scientific understanding of a flower and its parts, the dissection is pardonable. But is it the same in the analytical study of a human being? You get a perfect understanding of the individual, but what happens to the individual on the dissection couch?

Look! You Are a Victim!

People go for counseling when they come across problems in coping up with the living. They will try to handle their situations to the best of their abilities and it is only when they seem to fail they seek out counselors or anyone who would offer them comfort in their situation. Naturally normal counseling practices take on a problem-centered, problem-probing, problem-solving, person to person style of operations. The need for counseling is universally present in most human situations. Conflicts, doubts, confusion, pain, shame, anger, guilt, unforgiveness, frustrations and sufferings of the like are around in most circumstances as it always were.

Therefore the process of helping, encouraging, sustaining, supporting, teaching, comforting and so on were always present in all human societies in some form or the other. Mostly these functions were/are the province of religious leaders and in their teaching. Some of these ends were met by soothsayers, occult practitioners, witch doctors and con-artists of all descriptions.

Helping practices offering coping skills came to be known as counseling in our country about eighty or so years back, late in the 1950s, especially in the Christian circles. Psychology and Psychotherapy, the predecessor disciplines were here and there in the national scene, mostly in academic circles, mental institutions, less widely in general medical circuits about another hundred years before that. Thus in this country we may say the history of practice of psychology in its rudimentary form extends back to roughly about 150 years; approximately that is, while it was already in practice in the West for about 200 years since the time of Mesmer and Freud.

We refer to here the formal practice of 'counseling' as we understand it in the present social contexts. However, helping, guiding/misguiding, encouraging/ discouraging each other in love and concern and all the rest of the accepted counseling practice are not recent happenings. These were happening right from the beginning of the history of mankind. But once it took on the appearance of a therapy and started getting designated as 'counseling' with all the frills of psychotherapy it became a 'treatment discipline' centered on the client or the patient.

The 'client' who is not at ease is seriously concerned about the condition of the 'self' and so this 'self' seeks out ways to regain 'ease' or 'comfort'. The client is accepted as someone in trouble and is told not everything is fine with that 'self' because of all the emotional deprivation and wounds caused to it at various points in the life of the 'self'. Most popular counseling systems as practiced in our country and elsewhere make the 'self' the center point and a counselee is prepared to think in a pronounced 'self-centered' manner, which the therapist himself would call as the 'client-centered' therapy.

Right at the beginning of the counseling relationship, the counselor's concern is to make the client feel good, often to tell the client what she/he would love to hear. Seldom would a counselor exhibit the resolve to call a spade a spade. That takes a circuitous and tedious maze of leading questions to elicit answers and get across a suggestion that the counselor has formed within himself by that time.

One easy and welcome, practiced measure is to tell the client, "Yes, you have the problems; I understand your problems as you experience them. It is all caused by what you have gone through, your past and present circumstances. You were not responsible for what happened to you. Others in your life are responsible for your condition. We shall deal with it". For the client these or variations of these lines are nice to hear and gobble. It is so much better to hear that someone else is responsible for my problems. I am an innocent victim of circumstances and made such by people. No one wants to take on the blame on oneself for the mess that surrounds their lives. That is the point the professionals turn into a profitable proposition. The line they give out is made to be sweeter than the honeycomb, "You are a victim. You need help. We will provide it for consideration".

The tendency to run away from personal responsibility is widespread in all cultures. To say "you are responsible for my problems" is the most convenient soothing lie.

Many a saint was burned at the stake ascribing all evil happenings as his/her doings.

Some people go even beyond that. They think that if they do not find scapegoats, their plights will be precarious. The high priest had nothing much else to instigate his people to crucify Jesus. Blame-shifting is a fascinating game. "All my problems are because of you". Variations of this theme happen as a rule in most human interactions.

"Those who support me in my blame-shifting are my friends. I just love that person who says, "I am not to be blamed for my problems". I believe that person without questioning when he says that someone else in my past/present life is responsible for all my problems. If that person appears to be an expert in matters to do with the mind, I have no reason to distrust him. A psychologist adorning a robe as my savior, says I am a victim and he knows how exactly my parents and my peers damaged my self-esteem. Even before I say the details, the expert would know what all happened to me in the past. They are so smart and how can I disbelieve such all-knowing professionals? They hit the nail smack on the head that I have a poor opinion of myself or more precisely, I suffer from a low self-esteem syndrome caused in me by the rejecting people close to me. The revelation is so precise and intelligent in its finality.

"I am led to believe that I will feel like a failure, if I miss self-esteem. I am defeated and flattened and I think like a failure.

If at all I feel like escaping from my present beaten plight I must get professional help. I can be conditioned to think and act like a winner by expert mind-technicians, popularly called as the Psychotherapist, Psychologist, 'Counselor" or a 'Shrink' by some disrespectful people". Is it not closer to the expert's truth which I should savor and swallow?

A counselor should try to understand the complex mental transactions of the client, separating it into smaller components and getting a better grip before suggesting a wholesale panacea.

In the introduction to her book Manufacturing Victims, (described as a 'sizzling expose of the Psychology Industry' by eminent Psychology Professor Dr. Elizabeth Loftus, University of Washington) Dr.Tana Dineen Says:[20] "Psychology presents itself as a concerned and caring profession working with the good of its clients. But behind the benevolent façade is a voracious, self-serving industry that proffers facts which are often unfounded, provides therapy which can be damaging and exerts influence, which is having devastating effects on the social fabric".

Psychology has turned into a 'big-business'. It is no longer accurate to speak of it as a science and it is unscrupulously misleading to call it a profession. By and large, psychology has become an industry focused on self-interest and propelled by financial incentives. Unfortunately psychology's influence now extends across all aspects of life, telling us how to work, how to live, how to love and even how to play. We are confronted by psychologists expounding their theories on the endless list of TV talk shows, live broadcast news. "It is not news to say that psychology has become an influential cultural force or that society is becoming more and more filled with people who consider themselves victims; that it is doing this with motives based on power and profit".

[20]Tana Dineen, Manufacturing Victims (What psychology industry is doing to people), Robert Davies Multimedia 2000, pp.15, 17, 18.]

The discipline of Psychology has much to gain by convincing people they are victims and their present suffering is the doing of their parents, peers, immediate relatives, superiors and church and so on judging them wrong doers and sinners. It is no surprise after having created a huge market teaming with people who feel they are victims; psychology makes its silhouette sharper making it convenient for people to take refuge behind their lengthening shadow.

Moisturizers and Fairness creams have captured a sizable chunk of the cosmetic market after craftily creating a market by convincing people their good looks depend entirely on those products. The story of some expensive toothpastes and soaps are not different. These products publicize their touted essentiality 24x7. They easily convince and program people that their essential satisfaction and ultimate fulfillment for a life depend on the products. It means without making use of these products, you will be deprived of lasting satisfaction. We all know this is a business strategy but then many among us go and buy the very same products and some of us even go for lottery tickets too. You certainly have heard of the highly touted Neuro-Linguistic Programming. Commercial ads are NLP in real practice. The gullible among us largely support a lot of crooks without realizing the damage we do ourselves and others looking up to us.

We need to realize that the chief focus of psychological therapies is from a premise that the self is basically good but damaged by circumstances and others. That helps a large section of people who are in any sort of discomfort about themselves to think that they are in fact 'victims' because of the circumstances and the people they live with.

It is most tragic this waylaying happens in guiding people as to how they should live. The strategy is simple. People are led to believe their troubles lie out there – with others; but the truth is that solutions to the problems can be found within you, of course with our special knowledge and expert guidance. We are with you to help; "Our methods are the sure and best because it has 75 percent 'SIT' in it". (GOK, whatever that is!). So they fan up self-assertion, self-esteem, self-love, self-satisfaction, self-assertion, self-motivation, self-knowledge, self-excelling, self-worth, and self-fulfillment and so on. People do not ordinarily realize these self-centered acts drive them deeper into self-absorption, self-centeredness, self-indulgences, self-adoration and self-glorification which are anathema to Christian belief system. A Christian will do fine to know that "All have sinned and fallen short of the glory of God" (Rom. 3:23) and only God through the ministry of his Son Jesus Christ can reverse that situation and reconcile man with God.

A Christian meta-love-counselor stands to enable people to enter into a new life, reckoning them to be dead to sin and alive to God in Jesus Christ; made possible by the redeeming death of Jesus on the cross for the sins of all humanity. I take that you know the historic fact that Jesus, who knew no sin, took the sin of the whole world unto himself that he will give a new life to everyone who believes that he came from the Father to fulfill that commission. Jesus came to save sinners. I strongly hold that He did not come to help those who find comfort in holding others and their circumstances responsible for making them victims and pushing them to their present predicament.

The path of the cross distinctly stands out holding forth the ways to deal with serious matters of life. Our burdens are to be handed over to Him who is ready to take it from us and give us rest in return. (Mat.11: 28) Pain and suffering are realities of life and it is through these that we grow up to be whole persons, who are complete, perfect and lacking in nothing, with a firm standing in our Maker.

A Meta-love-counselor naturally and normally believes this irrefutable fact and lives by it to share his personhood in the love of Christ to those who are in all places without prejudice to individual differences. A Christian Meta-love-counselor is one who has appropriated his identity in Christ and turned a functional agent of transformation beyond the emotional, intellectual, volitional, spiritual aspects of human personality. He is supernaturally enabled to bring transcendence in the individual to be a whole person totally in the abounding grace of the Lord Jesus. This happens without the meta-love counselor being consciously aware of the change that happens in the person in need of healing. The meta-love-counselor is aware that the Lord is using her/

him in ways beyond her/his conscious understanding, and she/he is also aware of the transcendence that is happening. As is said elsewhere the Christian Meta-love-counselor is simply a presence in the light of the Supreme Omnipresence. Employing no counseling techniques, no commercial fixing, no psycho heresies, no monetary wrangling, no supervised leading, and no scientific abracadabra; the transcendence happens beyond human comprehension.

PETAL-7

COUNSELING VS COMFORT FIXING

Counseling and psychotherapy are familiar trades in any informed society. A person who is dissatisfied, not at ease within and without himself, because of internal or external reasons seeks out help. The person does not want any additional burden to what is already happening due to his/her own commissions or omissions. Taking on that additional responsibility is too much. He seeks after a quick release from the burden without having to own up the responsibility for it. The person is in need of 'ease' and desires an end to his 'dis-ease' condition. The ease-fixing industry of psychotherapy and its hundreds of variations are in the field to cater to this urgent need for 'ease' in persons experiencing 'dis-ease'. These 'feel-good'/comfort-fixing industries try to make people believe that all evils are due to causes outside of people. They maintain people are essentially good. Outside instances or individuals cause the bad they experience.

There are many factors contributing to the 'dis 'eases' of people. Such as economic circumstances, social environments, parents and parent figures, educational institutions, peer pressure, law enforcement agencies, violence in visual media, racial and sex discrimination, religious exploitation, filthy politics and filthier politicians, witchcraft by evil enemies, moral deterioration, falling value system, sexual permissiveness, globalization, influx of ungodly alien culture, religious fanaticism, and so on ad infinitum. Under such circumstances for the sake of keeping life going smooth, people have to adopt measures seen by others as evil. However, they are not supposed to be responsible for the evil they are compelled to commit. As we saw earlier, the defense is something or someone around one makes one do it. 'What I do is not evil, but as they are only some essential survival activities, is there any justification in designating my acts as evil?'

Indeed, what is evil and what is good? These definitions of evil and good are bound to be very subjective; they are relative. They differ according to circumstances and who makes the definitions and in what contexts. For instance, if a man rapes a minor girl because of the self-biased-impulsive-drives, that is not his fault. It happened because of the biases generated in the self by internal/external influences or conditions in the past or in the present. Is not a thief who steals, and if necessary kills for it, a product of social ills? No thief is a born thief. So goes the explanation.

The hue and cry made by moralists and conscience keepers is a pretension based on the assumption that people are basically sinful. That very idea is absurd. People are normally good. Training them to be good is superfluous and a demonstration of pretended arrogance of religions. That is the line taken by atheists and moral keepers of the society. It is obvious in these arguments that people need not to be changed. Their circumstances and social conditions are to be changed. Comfort fixers cash in on this thesis.

Thieves, pimps, killers, rapists, and corrupt leaders are all creations of the society. Unwed mothers and child prostitutes are the result of improper sex education. HIV+ and AIDS are so widespread because not enough condoms are provided wherever they are needed. Providing condoms is the most effective way to stem the onslaught of AIDS according to government officials. Society has the responsibility to create awareness in people about all these matters. Why hold the rapist or sex-worker or their patrons responsible for their actions? Are they not products of society and their upbringing?

Where reasoning of this sort is prevalent and encouraged, more and more killer rapists come out boldly defying social systems and mores. Perpetrators of evil are defended and exonerated by the parties they belong to and through smart lawyers. They multiply exponentially, and they are quite comfortable in their operations and often aided by leaders of grey shades.

If they are caught by some chance, some of those criminals are punished occasionally depending on the financial, social influence of the victim's people. However, often justice remains conveniently concealed in law books. Do grimed hands thwart it? Your guess is as good as mine is. The smart ones who do not get caught make life tedious for themselves and others bringing down a curse onto the society. Declared lawbreakers are not the only ones who bring out the larger chunk of social evil. Just ordinary people like you and I do that. We who strive to produce personal comfort ignoring the well-being of others are the major culprits. When 'comfort at any cost' becomes the creed of ordinary people, misery is duplicated closer to home. Then there are many who go about breeding evil and remain unseen both in splinter and large political parties. The few who perchance realize there is something wrong with them and see that they are missing 'ease' despite their best efforts opt for fixing-up of some sort. They too become fodder for the 'feel-good' mood-fixing industries. Now tell me if there is any truth in these lines below;

> [1] "... ...even though every inclination of his heart is evil from childhood" (Gen 8:21).
>
> [2] A fool finds pleasure in evil conduct (Prov. 10:23).
>
> [3] Evil comes to him who searches for it (Prov. 11:27).
>
> [4] Woe to those who call evil good and good evil... ....(Isa 5:20).
>
> [5] "... ....wash the evil from your heart to be saved" (Jer. 4:14).
>
> [6] "...so turn from your evil ways, each one of you and reform your ways..." (Jer. 18:11).

[7] "….. Do not use your freedom as a cover-up for evil" (1 Pet. 2:16).

[8] "……all the evil doers are full of boasting (Ps. 94:4).

[9] "… … our sins are higher than our heads….." (Ezra. 9:6).

[10] "He who conceals his sins does not prosper… ….(Prov. 28:13).

[11] "….I acknowledged my sin to you (Ps. 32:5).

[12] "…..for there is no one who does not sin….." (I Kings. 8:46).

[13] ….. and be sure that your sin will find you" (Num. 32:23).

[14] "…..for all have sinned and fallen short of the glory of God (Rom. 3:23).

There are many more verses and statements that affirm the basic sinfulness of man. Sinful thoughts and acts of men contend for deriving gratification in all situations, to gain that 'feeling good' state, which is the preferred comfort zone. Apart from accidents, contagious illnesses, natural calamities, genetic aberrations and willful suffering, all pains are the results of wrong individual reactions to life and life situations. Wrong reactions and false coping may be due to ignorance or willful refusal of godly, loving, understanding responses to life and life situations.

When men and women react wrongly to life situations, they tarnish their image further, beyond that which has already happened in Adam. Their anger, anxiety, fears, guilt, unforgiveness, pride, lust, impatience, greed, addictions and so on, distort them so much they become less than them. They become less than whole, to say the least!. They shatter the inbuilt integrated wholeness. This topic demands larger detailed study.

Jesus asked the paralytic at the pool of Bethesda 'Do you want to be whole?'

Restoration of integrated wholeness through transformation in man is a definite part of the counseling ministry. Healing happens as wholeness is restored and the individual transformed. The original distortion that happened in Adam not only has to be restored but the Adamic life has to be transformed to Christ-life. That is where Christian counseling has its relevance. It is not some sort of fixing. It is a transformation clear and clean to the point that one should be able to say, 'I no longer live' meaning the old 'Adamic' 'I' that I was, no longer live, but Christ lives in me. It is restoration of wholeness through total transformation of the depraved. It further means transformation is by the only One who is whole! It echoes Paul's declaration in[34] Galatians 2:20 "I have been crucified with Christ; I no longer live... ..."

Jesus transforms. He makes all things new. In Him, all things become new and the old passes away.[35] 2 Corinthians 5:17

makes it amply obvious to all. Therefore if any man is in Christ, he is a new creation: old things have passed away; behold all things have become new. In that state of newness, the transformed person is dead to the past and[36] that life is hidden with Christ in God (Col. 3:3). That person will no longer conform to the world but would be open[37] by the mercies of God to present his body as a living sacrifice, acceptable to God (Rom 12:1-2).

PETAL-8

COUNSELING USED AS A MONEY-SPINNER

Most counseling practices including some Christian varieties have turned their focus on how to make personal gains through this service. For a counselor, counseling is counted as a ministry of love; a calling. But that aspect takes a less important role when the question of a fee comes up. The higher the profile of the counselor, naturally higher the fee, that is the going truth.

India is a country with many faiths. All major religions are represented in this land. Let us have a look at the positions our religions hold on making personal gains.

The Zoroastrian faith holds that[38]– "Someone of small possessions here below inclines into the truth but who so has great riches is unfortunate, O Lord" (Zen Avesta 47:4). This clearly does not advocate love for riches or money.

Sikhism holds;[39] "The God-instructed are truly joyful, the egoists miserable. The divine vision to the God-instructed is manifest; from the egoist turned away. The God-instructed are truly untied. To the God-instructed is known the path of renunciation" (Gurugrandh Sahib).

This is not advocating the path of amassing possessions or money.

Buddhism;[40] "When after becoming enlightened, inspired by the spirit of self-discipline, a person proceeds to renounce the world and embrace asceticism that person's parents to begin to lament – but the enlightened one does not go back" (The Acaranga Sutra 6: 26, 27, 27, 28, 29).[41] There is no indication to go after possessions here. "Leaving behind the path of darkness and following the path of light let the wise person leave home life and go into life of freedom. In solitude that few enjoy, find your joy supreme" (Dhammapada. 6: 87–89).

Islam; The emphasis is on leaving everything; not hoarding[42]. "Righteousness does not consist in where, whether you face towards the East or West. Righteous one is one who believes in Allah – who for the love of Allah gives wealth to kinsfolk, orphans, the needy, the wayfarers and the beggars – such are the true believers; such are the God-fearing" (The Holy Koran 2:177).

It is recommending sharing, giving away wealth.

Hinduism:[43] Whosoever in work finds silence, and sees that silence is work, sees indeed the light and in all works finds peace. Such a one expects nothing, relies on nothing, and even has fullness of joy. These people have no vain hopes, they are masters of their souls, they surrender all they have, only the body works; they are free (Bhagavad Gita).

This is not hankering after anything, only surrendering.

Christianity:[44] "Blessed are you who are poor, for yours is the kingdom of God"(Holy Bible, Luke 6:20)

The prompting is to seek the kingdom of heaven and not riches.

All major religions and their values teach not to itch for wealth. All the major Scriptures have references which talk about the traps in seeking after wealth, affluence and power. From these teachings helping professionals have drifted far afield. Our schools are churning out the 'educated' to seek wealth beyond security. Every enterprise is geared to rake in money. The ethos of the 'counseling industry', a relatively new arrival in the service scene also is the same. It is no wonder that the Christian variety of counseling too is much of a business proposition with structured fee and stuff.

I want you to think and ask yourself the simple question; "Would money-making be the primary goal in Meta-love-counseling?" Jesus says to us, "Freely you have received, freely give". Where would we offer a hiding place for Jesus in our counseling set-up?

Think of Christian perfection as perfection in love, especially forgiving love.[45] Matt. 5:44-48: "...love your enemies, bless those who curse you, do good to those who hate you, and pray for those who spitefully use you and persecute you, that you may be sons of your Father in heaven; for He makes His sun rise on the evil and on the good, and sends rain on the just and on the unjust.... Therefore you shall be perfect, just as your Father in heaven is perfect." The Christian Meta-love-counselor's prayer should be; *Lord Jesus, I trust you for grace to be perfected in Your love.*

Quote:[46] "To live by faith is to live in humility, in patience, long-suffering, obedience, resignation, absolute trust and dependence upon God, with all that is temporal and earthly under our feet." — William Law, *'The Power of the Spirit'*

[47] Read again 2 Corinthians 1:3-4 in first-person singular and think yet again and decide whether we have any justification in charging a fee. But then how would the Christian Meta-love-counselor survive without a means to live?

That is a very legitimate question and my answer to that:

1. Helping, encouraging, sustaining, guiding and the like are Christian responsibilities to others. It is a ministry that the Christian community owes to its members. Therefore, the Christian, Meta-love-counselor should be supported by the Christian community. The church should send out the 'angels of mercy' to minister among the people in need. Somehow the churches are unlikely to see this aspect of Christian Meta-love-counseling ministry. That may be a wrong assumption on my part as there are examples of churches with deeper concerns for their members.

2. The meta-love-counselor will not be justified in stipulating and receiving a structured fee, but if the counselee out of gratitude for the help received offers a love gift, the Meta-love-counselor shall accept it. There should be no expectation of any sort in this. The point is in honoring the counselor with a gift, some counselees would find a sense of satisfaction in giving. We have no right to deny that to the counselee and that should not be considered and receiving remuneration of any kind. The Met-love-counselor rejoices in the sharing of the comfort he receives from the Father. If the Father prompts the heart of the counselee to 'give', the Meta-love-counselor shall gracefully 'receive' it.
3. Those who have an independent means of income and who are constrained by the love of Christ should accept Meta-love-counseling as a ministry and be a blessing, using their own resources to comfort others in need. This ultimately is the counselor's best means of glorifying God.

PETAL-9

COUNSELOR QUALITIES

Let me restate the position this book is taking. Counseling a person in suffering and pain is not about a lot of things done to that person. In fact, it is not about doing things. As a community, Christians have come to be program-oriented in a big way. Perhaps we are not different in this from everyone else. We are very good in defining, designing, drafting, describing, detailing, differentiating and by and large destroying the divine elements in what we used to call the Divine ministries. However, at this point we need to look at the counseling ministry with a fresh departure from those in commercial enterprises. Enterprises, in course of time, would turn into industries if they have to survive as profit making outfits. But counseling is about being a blessing in the life of the person, as an instrument of blessings from above with no entrepreneur agenda. Our God is not a God of programs. There are times as counselors we would be at our wits end. It is when we are weak that He acts. His power is manifested when we are at our weakest. God reassures us not to be perturbed or exasperated. When we come to a grinding halt and are not even able to articulate a prayer, He is there waiting to bless us and use us, whispering in our ears, "My grace is sufficient for you: ". We are utterly unworthy yet we are called out to represent Him to the broken person as His instrument. An instrument has to be in prime condition, sharpened, honed, fitted and right.

There are obvious qualities that enhance the usability of an instrument. When applied to a servant of the all-giving God the variety is infinite in the provisions of the great Giver. We look at some of it in our limited reach.

1. Abiding holiness

Abiding is a boundless privilege. The invitation to come into abiding in the holy living God through His Son is an unimaginably awesome privilege. To approach the flaming holiness of the Almighty, the all-consuming God, any uncleanliness would be a blockage. One has to receive holiness from the gracious Father before venturing it.

'Be holy as I am holy' is not a command that a Christian counselor can afford to ignore or take casually. There is nothing to be unduly worried about it because

[48] His words make us clean (John 15:3). By confessing our sinfulness and believing in His faithfulness to forgive,[49] we become cleansed (1 John 1:9). As we abide in His word and enter into a body-mind-spirit-love relationship with Him, an organic abiding becomes the natural outcome.[50] Every

person has spirit, mind (soul) and body, constituting the whole person (1. Thes. 5:23).

Relating with at least one aspect of the organism to another entity becomes an organic connection. In grafting a scion with a stock, an organic relationship is established in the physical sense. Two people putting their heads together and making choices is an organic relating in a larger soul (mental) sense. In an even larger expanded spiritual sense, a spiritual relating of man with his God also qualifies to be an organic connection. Abiding in the True Vine as its bench is essentially an organic relating in that spiritual sense too. This may appear wild theorizing, but it is perfectly within the offer of abiding that Jesus makes in John 15. You need to be a fool to accept this!

Are you too proud to be a fool for Christ Jesus?

2. Humility

We cannot approach claiming a right to abide. Abiding is not barging in to execute a claim forcibly. With Jesus, the first is the last and the last the first. He calls for humility through His object examples. It has been specifically laid out; to come into any blessing we must know[51] and do as He did in all humility (John 13:17). He told us He came to man to serve him[52] and to give His life for man (Matt 20:28). The ungodly lord it over others. As His servant, the Christian-meta-love-counselor is expected to be[52] a humble servant (1 Pet 2:2-3), taking the very nature of a servant[53] as Jesus did (Phil 2:7),[54] serving one another in love (Gal 5:13), bearing the burdens of others (Gal 6:2) If anyone has anything to do in the name of Jesus, that person should first of all have the humility of Jesus to being one with Him.

A proud, conceited, spiritually arrogant prig of a Pharisee who goes to church every Sunday and takes the seat of importance in fellowships, heading every church committee, who loudly shouts moral exhortations to all and sundry is not Jesus' idea of a servant counselor. That is what I tend to think. I am inclined to believe I am not far from the truth here. There is an old saying that water would only flow to lower ground. Blessings are not shot up. They come down in showers.

3. Gentleness

(Long-suffering- in-forgiveness). The one who seeks our help is called to abide into the One who is gentle and[54] humble in heart (Matt 11:28, 29, 30), where rest to the soul of the abiding one is promised. To be worthy of the calling to be a servant, we are exhorted to be[55] completely humble and gentle, patient, bearing with one another (Eph. 4:2). The prospective adherent must have a gentleness that is demonstrably evident in him for all to see.[56] 'Let your gentleness be known to all' says Paul (Phil 4:5).

The abiding counselor is in a position to lead the potential counselee to wholeness. He is to have all the qualities of a leader. Paul lays down these qualities as, above reproach, the husband of but one wife, temperate, self-controlled, respectable, hospitable, and able to teach, not given to drunkenness, not violent but gentle, not quarrelsome,[57] not a lover of money

(1 Tim 3:3). Then Peter mentions[58] the unfading beauty of a gentle and quiet spirit (1 Pet 3:4). The Christian counselor is expected to function in an apostolic style described by[59] Paul in 2 Corinthians 10:1: By the meekness and gentleness of Christ. That gentleness is contagious. It produces a 'morphic-resonance' of gentleness in those who are counseled by the gentle counselor. That makes counseling a positive blessing. A rude, arrogant, conceited, pushy, manipulative Christian counselor is an oxymoron and indeed a perfect moron too!

Counselor! You please take specific note of the fact that you can give only what you have. If you are not a gentle person you would not be the right person to infuse gentleness in others.

4. Forgiveness

Only a forgiving person can find identification with someone who is the epitome of forgiveness. The whole purpose of the life of Jesus on earth was to offer forgiveness to humankind. Jesus laid great emphasis on forgiving and taught his disciples forgiveness as one thing required of them as they go into prayer to the Father. Forgiveness is the only thing that we need to contribute to be at the receiving end of God's provisions. After teaching to pray, Lord Jesus took extra effort to explain the significance of[60] forgiving (Matt 6:14, 15).[61] 'Forgive and your will be forgiven' (Luke. 6:37).[62] Forgive as the Lord forgave you (Col 3:13). This is one effective way to strike a bonding with anyone to whom we want to relate. An unforgiving counselor is an incongruity. An unforgiving individual is a hardened, disconnected, far off island on fire. The fire is not visible to the distant mainland dwellers that have their own fires to tend. There are no bridges. This individual is a loner. He has come to you for a cooling down of his heart smoldering in unforgiveness. One of the early responsibilities of the Christian counselor is to help build the first tentative bridge for the hardened individual. Help him/her to take the first trip in forgiveness toward another individual. An unforgiving individual does not earn forgiveness. As an unforgiven individual, that individual does not forgive. The truth that we all need to get hold of is that forgiveness is found free in Jesus. Are you, as a counselor in the making, a forgiven person? If not you need to get down on your knees and receive it from the Father.

5. Patience

The Lord God is forgiving. His forgiveness is because of His patience with the sinful ways of man. Many evils man commits are because of the lack of patience. An individual in a hurry has no time to think about the consequences of an act. Quick gratification does not allow for a considered response. The force of the position 'I must get' is huge, ready to smash any obstacle in its path. Forceful emotional thrusts more often guide the way he reacts. Discrimination would be absent because highly charged emotional acts are usually illogical. If such acts were described as unreasonable it would not be widely off the mark. Hurting one's own flesh and blood, going even to the extreme of destroying others, is a common sight. Where that happens there is inevitable distortion in perception and reaction. Man would then be more likely to act in a zoological manner than acting as human beings. An individual acting as a zoological entity is not subject to any moral constraints. Many of the atrocious acts in times of war and even during peace will not occur if man rises above the cannibalistic, animal inclinations. An unthinking individual is not able to make the right decision and has no power over any of the strong emotions like fear, anger, anxiety, guilt, envy, lust, shame, etc. In highly charged states, the unthinking person commits many sins and makes himself/herself unworthy of God. Without patience an abiding rest is impractical. A restless heart in a counselor is counterproductive, breeding only more confusion and conflicts in the counselee.

Wait on the Lord. Your heart is His abode. His lap is where your head reclines. Be in touch with Jesus and sense His validating presence to be equal to the awesome responsibility assigned to you in caring for a precious soul directed to you by Him. The person you counsel is not there by accident. He is sent. Do have the patience to lead him to what he is seeking, peace and rest!

6. Availability

Rush, rush and be done with, the faster the better! Quick fixes are the norm of the day. Think of the response of Jesus to the centurion who came to Jesus for healing for his ailing servant at home. Without bothering to enquire about how distant the place was or how to get to the place he simply said, 'I will come'. That is what suffering people want to hear from you, that 'I am available to be with you in your pain'. The individual in pain is scanning for a listening heart, a shoulder to cry on, a comforting and unhurried pat on the shoulder. 'Tell me, I am here to listen to your pain. I am willing to walk along with you. Take your time to gather your thoughts. I will wait with you'. Such an approach is a soothing balm. The meta-love-counselor owes it to the person in pain. Otherwise, the meta-love-counselor reduces himself to something less than an ordinary counselor; he then adorns the garb of a professional dealing in commercial lines. A Christian cannot afford to be that crassly base. We need to remember that counseling is a calling, a ministry, not a business enterprise. Structured and efficacious dealing, shuffling out stereotyped answers even to the palpable pains of people can only be termed as nothing less than contempt, mocking the humanity of the person in suffering.

Another detail the meta-love-counselor should be aware of is the fact of the nearness of Jesus when counseling is done in His name. Where the counselor and counselee are together in His name, He is right in the midst of them as He promises. Jesus makes Himself available to those in pain. The meta-love-counselor has to apportion time wisely to be available to the counselee in a rush-free setting. Rush takes away the joy in fellowship. I do not suggest fellowships should be bracketed with counseling. Most often subjectivity and sympathy rightly rule Christian fellowships. That is a beautiful thing. But in counseling, the counselee needs an understanding person with a degree of unhurried objectivity to discern the intricacies of the issues involved. You owe that to your counselee in interpathy.

7. Servant hood.

It is the extension of the quality of humility we referred to earlier, yet it goes a step further. Humility often is a deep inner attitude that reassuringly reflects in interpersonal dealings. It is acknowledging others as no less than oneself and accepting oneself as a product of grace. Humility that makes itself a visible piece of a benevolent exhibit is camouflaged pride, deceitful pretension. A servant is willing to be on the knees and wash the feet that are dirty even without and before being asked. The servant without being prompted takes on to him what needs to be done! His service is as service to the Lord, not to please anyone in particular.

Servant hood is not far removed from stewardship. In both, there is accountability to the Master. In Christian meta-love-counseling/guidance, Christ Jesus calls the counselor/guide to be the available servant to the needy. The counselor /guide is the extended arm of Jesus to share the peace and rest that he receives from the real Healer. The servant is sensitive to the need not only in the Body of Christ, but also in every locus of need without distinction.

We need to have a larger understanding of servant hood in the biblical context. The modern and secular concept of servant hood is that in compliance of the organized work force signing the dotted lines of a union leadership, doing what is required of the servant by the set rules of the institution or orders from an individual. It has its beneficial aspect for an organized labor force. Biblical servant hood is far removed from this political agenda.

Jesus Christ the servant king came to do the will of His Father. Pleasing the Father was His only concern, to the point of giving himself up. What I am implying is a similar sense of commitment in the meta-love-counselor/guide, as impossible as that might appear. This would appear as too idealistic, but within the range of possibilities in Jesus we would see this happen in His grace and grace alone.

8. Not conforming to the world

A Christian meta-love-counselor/guide is called to minister to the total needs of the person and lead that person to wholeness in Christ. Take along that person in the paths of righteousness where that person would have a chance to have the total[63] joy that is promised in Jesus (John 15:11). Someone who is wedded to the standards and ways of the world will not be able to do this. The world system of counseling beefs up the self and trains people to find their comfort zones to feel the type of superficial elation they are looking for. Deeper matters of the spirit are not the world's cup of tea. A Christian counselor/guide has to have a commitment deeper and greater than the superficial commitment of the abjectly worldly counselor.

What the world offers is tickling stuff appealing to the senses, desirable to satiate the need for gratification. Our senses are sharply tuned to wavelengths of the worldly offers. The path to gratification is wide and smooth, preferred at first sight by those who have no finger to hold on to. Be a counselor who has his index finger not dipped in the stagnant poison pots of the world but free on offer to lead along the stranded and wounded to the pinnacle of their possibilities.

'Therefore I urge you, brothers, in view of God's mercy, to offer your bodies as living sacrifices, holy and pleasing to God – this is your spiritual act of worship.

[64]Do not conform any longer to the pattern of this world' (Rom 12:1,:2). This exhortation needs to be acknowledged by all as a specific directive to a prospective Christian meta-love- counselor /guide.

9. Non-judging, accepting

A Christian meta-love-counselor guide is one who secures release for people trapped within themselves. The help seekers in some ways may be blind to the truth. Too often they make prisoners of themselves in their finite thinking, limited perceptions and distorted definitions in life. A Christian counselor/guide needs to be wiser about the ways in which people build up concentric rings of insulation around themselves in an effort to evade criticism. They tend to move away from people, fearing rejection.

They come to prefer isolation because there is less possibility of disapproval at a distance. Even as they yearn to embrace, they wrestle to be dispelling proximity. In their eagerness to feel fine, they have ended up doing many apparently foolish things. We do not have to offer approval of their acts. However, the suffering of the person in suffering warrants recognition. A practicing Christian, the Christian counselor /guide has no right to disapprove of the sinner. There is a potential saint in every sinner. Love the sinner but certainly disapprove of the sin and sinful ways. The counselor /guide offers acceptance based on the disarming acceptance he himself receives from his Savior. The Lord's non-judgmental acceptance of the woman of the street in John 8 is an objective example for the Christian counselor /guide to follow. 'Neither do I condemn you' is a line that should reverberate in the ears of a Christian counselor dealing with the so-called failed lives. To be not standing in judgment the counselor has to have a sense of who he is. He must have had the right answer to the question. 'Who am I?' If I am comfortable with identification with my achievements, accomplishments, adulations and accumulated possession; then I stand in danger of judging others by those standards. I then get a faulty picture, and I make a faulty judgment which would color my whole relationship with the person I counsel. Go even further and be certain that you do not judge anyone by any set standards. Confidentially, who are you to judge others? Do not give the Lord an occasion to ask you that harsh question!

10. Sense of equality

This is very close to the point we just discussed. No one is lesser than another one. By the same standard, none is greater than another is. Christ died for all. The price paid for each person is the same. He paid with His blood for you, for me, for every person on planet earth. None is bigger than any other by that standard. The love of God and the active grace in Him constrain the counselor /guide to help a helpless person in trouble. Flouting this great principle has caused untold misery in the world.

Slave trade, apartheid, untouchables, ethnic wars, any war for that matter are all variants of this theme. Skin color, fire-power and brutal majority make some people more equal than others. As you feel, I too am indignant. Leading along and helping a person to know her/his potential for outgrowing her/his present problems in God's provisions is a privilege, not a license to dictate. Christian help offered is always from a platform of equality. Unless the Christian counselor glimpses the image of God in each person he deals with, he is on a private trip to personal gain. An exploitative 'big-brother' strategy is a disgrace to any Christian service. Physical circumstances might give some people an idea that there are people who are lesser than others are. This is part of the frivolous pretensions of the middle class mediocrity. The Christian counselor/ guide cannot indulge in that sort of immaturity.

No one would appreciate sermonizing down from a high perch. This is very serious professional hazard with practicing Christians. Some pious Christians have a fixation that it is hard for all and sundry to gain entry to heaven, which is reserved for the 144,000 who belong to their particular denomination. It would be ugly to stretch it any further.[65] Galatians 3:26–29 would be one refreshing idea in this respect.

You are all sons of God through faith in Christ Jesus, for all of you who were baptized into Christ have clothed yourselves with Christ. There is neither Jew nor Greek, slave nor free, male nor female, for you are all one in Christ Jesus. If you belong to Christ, then you are Abraham's seed, and heirs according to the promise.

11. Discerning

Another basic and essential requirement in Christian counseling /guiding is the deep awareness that the True Counselor is the Holy Spirit and not any human agency.

The Christian counselor/guide is only an instrument at the disposal of the Holy Spirit. The counselor is used by the Holy Spirit for spreading blessing in the lives of those who are in trouble. The counselor is the extended blessing arm of his God, the Comforter and Healer. The counselor comforts all others in any manner of trouble by the comfort with which he himself is comforted by the Father of all comforts. This is the bottom line in Christian counseling.

A counselor needs to ask a standard question of one's own self when dealing with a person in need for physical, emotional, spiritual support. 'Do I see the potential saint in this person?' Then be able to see that saint and relate as to a potential saint. The Lord saw a potential saint in the sinful woman who wept at His feet in the house of Simeon the Pharisee. All the people around in the banquet only saw her history and murmured against her. Only the Lord saw the saint in her. I believe this is the kind of discerning which Christ expects us to possess.

Discerning is an inspired happening. A discerning counselor apart from being patient, available, forgiving, accepting and so on should have the grace to listen to the Holy Spirit more than he/she listens to the mumbling of his/her own heart. I do not say this denigrating the wise personal inferences of a counselor. They have their pertinent relevance as an intellectual activity. Christian counseling has a dimension beyond intelligent inferences. I believe divine wisdom happens in the interface of knowledge and faith. That is the general area where intuition and discerning arise.

Intuition is the internally revealed certainty. Often people come with intellectual problems seeking rational solutions.

More often than not, a great number of these people have moral problems they are at effort to mask. There would be forceful suggestions from the counselor's intelligence and experience that would be enough to arrive at the facts. I have no problem with that argument. But I can assure you with the backing of 50 years of assorted counseling experience that you would be surprised at the discerning the Holy Spirit reveals. You would be better off in the care of the Holy Spirit.

12. Assurance

People who come to seek comfort and consolation exist on shaky and hopeless frames of the inner environment. Stabilize them with hope and bright expectations of the unfailing love of God and ultimate freedom from their problems as they put their trust in God. The counselor /guide has to have a sincerely fine tuned vocabulary of positive hope and assurance. The ordinary inclination to pacify people in pain through superficial platitudes is a cruel mockery of their vulnerability. The credibility of the hope that is in Christ should get across to the people through the genuine and informed assurance reflected in the words and attitudes of the Christian counselor.

There is a tremendous lot of composure and peace emanating from a genuine person in an abiding relationship with the Lord Jesus Christ.

The genuine person, the Christian counselor, has the unshakable confidence in[66] Romans 8:26–28: 'In the same way the Spirit also helps us in our weakness. We do not know how to pray as we should, but the Spirit Himself intercedes for us with groaning too deep for words; and he who searches the hearts knows what the mind of the Spirit is, because He intercedes for the saints according to the will of God. And we know that God causes all things to work together for good to those who love God, to those who are called according to His purpose'.

This assurance is not on display nor is it flaunted in a holier-than-thou-attitude. Yet it passes on despite the abiding person. Every word, the very look, every muscle in the face and body is a stamp of assurance to the person struggling in doubt and indecision. Doubt, indecision, fear, anger, guilt and emotions of that species are the marks of a person who misses assurance. That person may be in the throes of rejection too. 'I have no one. No one loves me. No one wants me. I am no good' are the dominant thoughts in a rejected person.

When dealing with such rejected persons, the counselor has to ask himself a few pertinent questions:-

Do I have a;

> A heart that unconditionally accepts and not arrogant,
>
> A heart that believes fully in God only and not doubting,
>
> A heart that expressly blesses and never blaming,
>
> A heart the genuinely cares for others and not cursing,

A heart that holds its dignity and not disturbing,

A heart that encourages and not enfeebling,

A heart that freely forgives and not given to fighting,

A heart that is humble and never haughty,

A heart that inspires not inhibiting,

A heart that is joyful not judgmental,

A heart that is equally kind to all not kicking all and sundry,

A heart that loves the unlovable but not lusting after,

A heart that is motivated to mend with no malice toward any,

A heart that is noble in its disposition never negating anyone,

A heart that is disarmingly open and not obstinate,

A heart that pleases God and never given to pride,

A heart that manifests quietness of spirit and not quarrelsome,

A heart that is rested and not rushed,

A heart that is self-less and surrendered; not self-seeking,

A heart that is always thankful to God, not troubled,

A heart that does understand, not uncaring,

A heart that validates others, never violating any,

A heart that is warm in dealings never planning wrongdoings

A heart that is yielded to Love not yelling vengeance,

A heart that has the zest for blessing and not given to zealotry.

The list of qualities is bound to be a long one. We mention only the very basic ones.

As we approach the awesome presence of God, we begin to receive grace that will open our eyes to our glaring deficiencies in many areas of our lives. However, we have to make a beginning and God is someone who knows us inside out and all our weaknesses and sinfulness. When we approach Him in repentance and faith, He is righteous enough to cleanse us from all our unrighteousness. In the blessed state of oneness with the whole person, sinless and perfect that Jesus is, wholly God and wholly man, we have hope for healing and wholeness, which we would be able to pass on. He told us to love each other, in line with the original command. As we keep his commands, we live deeply and surely in him, and he lives in us purifying us.[67] (1 John 3:3)

PETAL-10

DISTORTIONS

Largely we refuse to see or ignore the distortions that happen in gross measure all around us. Distortions lead to disintegration in time. A disintegrating individual may lay put even beyond 38 years if someone does not come along and ask that individual 'Do you want to be whole?' The technician who sits in a counseling office does not have the motivation or total assurance to ask that question. His 'victims' are supposed to come to his office and pay the registration fee prior to consultation. Some non-ignorable facts stare at us in our faces.

One cannot but help to notice the increase in tension, suffering, suicides, substance abuse, etc., on one side and proportionate increase in literacy, advance in technology, GNP, Per-capita income on the other. General increases in prosperity for some push down many more below the line of poverty. An increase in unrighteousness proportionately increases the number of people existing below the Line of Desperation (L o D). Who has the time and disposition to go searching for those below the lines? Because our subject here is not poverty but desperation, let us deal with the L o D later.

Let me try to explain this point. The unrighteous live for gratifying their desires. As long as their evil desires remain fulfilled they maintain a low profile. However, they will not remain that way for long because their desires grow bigger and bigger. They want to fill themselves with the things and people they desire. They do not always get their way. Setbacks upset them. Thoughts of failure and desires that are most forceful make their lives miserable, and they get heavily laden with distress, displeasure and 'dis-ease'. Inevitably, they sink down below the 'Line of Desperation'-(L o D). The unrighteous, pushing their desires and having a ball for the moment, manage to cling onto jolly sensations, fancy they remain above the line of desperation fooling them for the interim and long-term when actively assisted by higher-ups. Those who straightaway get depressed in a plethora of worldly concerns and frustrated desires with their heavily laden hearts sink to the bottom and remain below the L o D.

These two groups have a proportional relationship. The feed bank for those below is the righteous multitude who manages to remain on top for the moment although they can never stay up permanently. The final destination for those who perpetrate unrighteousness is without doubt below the L o D. Who can lift man above the L o D and give him hope? Who can take man out of the predicament of his own making?

The Lord Jesus specifically asks us to give Him all our burdens that make us sink to the levels below the Lo D to Him. As we give away the burdens to Him, we become lighter and gain a certain degree of buoyancy to let us rise up above the Lo D. Only the Lord Jesus who takes away our burdens can lift us above the Lo D where we enjoy the freedom to rejoice in the oneness with the Redeemer. In this context, we need to remember and discern the significance of what the Lord Jesus said elsewhere in[68] Matthew 10:39, 'He who has found his life shall lose it, and he who has lost his life for My sake shall find it'. Too many concerns make us heavy; giving it up to the Lord takes away the burdens leading to freedom from all bondages that keep us bound and stranded in the depths.

Not many dwelling in sin would want to shout out and cry for help. There is addictive pleasure carrying on in sin and spreading unrighteousness. 'What is the hue and cry for? We are not hurting anyone! We just try to make life livable'. They, in fact, would want to maintain that other individuals and instances push them into their predicament. They have no problem at all in warming up to people who agree with their claim of being victims of circumstances. You would find an abundance of professionals singing to this tune and making a quick buck in the stinking bargain.

Young and old people come to me for sharing their experiences and invariably all the time expecting me to support them in their claims and findings that others are at fault for their suffering

Some examples:

George, 47, father of 3 and self-employed as insurance agent, has a strong suicidal urge. According to him, this was due to the angry outburst of his father during student days, telling him 'you are a no good bum'.

(You see! My father is causing the problem)

Leela, 38, married and childless, has extramarital inclinations. This, she says, is because her mother never really loved her father, and she was always angry with her mother. She is taking it out on her mother.

(Mother is responsible)

Navin, 21, failed three times in his final CA examination and stopped studies because his mother always had unrealistic expectations and compared him with his cousins.

(Mother! Who else is responsible?)

Joseph, 41, hardware merchant, has taken to alcohol in a big way because his partners have cheated him in business. Not only that, his wife keeps accusing him.

(Partners and wife together are responsible)

Aslam, 53, and a grandfather, has according to him 'great love for servants' and he invariably ends up in bed with every maid servant because his father set examples for him.

(Of course, father is the cause!)

Jayadevan, 65, also has the same problem, but he says he has to be kind to house-maids because his parents were stingy and harsh to servants.

(Both parents pushed him to this)

Nimmi, 23, and unmarried, had had three abortions already because she was a rich, lonely child who grew up in hostels most of her student days.

(All girls in hostels should get pregnant and abort because their parents choose to send them to hostels. What else can they do?)

Lalitha, 16; 12th standard student, steals money from her roommates because her parents never give her enough money.

(Doesn't she have a right to steal because of what her parents have done?)

Pushkaran, 19, was 'caught copying' in his BSc 2nd year examination. He says it was the fear of his father's wrath that prompted him to do that.

(You are right, Pushk; your father is the cause!)

Gaffer, 30, was forced to beat up his mom because she was always nasty to his 'poor' father.

(Who else will discipline the mother?)

Mary, 13, stopped going to church seeing that her mother, an inveterate churchgoer, was unkind to beggars.

(Mother is wrong, not me!)

Narayaniamma, 67, a widow for a long number of years, insists her newly married son keep his bedroom door open because her father and her husband had early deaths.

(Honest to God, it is only because they died early that I do this)

Deepika, 28, an ex-air hostess and a Karate black belt, beat up her husband because her father-in-law has ignoble intentions towards her.

(Son of a father like that deserves this)

Sajeev, 27, does not want to go for his interview to be chef in a big hotel because his friends discourage him obliquely indicating he is not good. They also say he is obese and only wants access to good food.

(People are so unkind)

Joseph, an IT Professional, has been sending his 10-year-old perfectly normal daughter to a psychiatrist for the last two years because his wife has a psychiatric condition.

(I have got to be cautious; I do not want my child to turn psychotic)

Natarajan, 39, cannot stop talking even after hours of yakking corrective instructions to his 26-year-old wife of four years to correct her. Her husband beats her, she says besides he is a cruel man.

(Short of hitting her verbally and physically, what else can Natarajan do?)

The individuals concerned in every one of these instances do not believe they are responsible for whatever is happening.

Their present/past circumstances/experiences compel them to such acts. They remain desperate and sunk in depression blaming anyone and everyone in sight.

"How can anyone in their right sense blame me for what I do to cope up best with life as I experience it?" Answer to this specific question is readymade. Practically every counseling module bases its constructs on the understanding that things happen to people without their causing it. What happens to people is not their responsibility. They are just victims of circumstances. That is a lovely thing to hear. I certainly would be happy to be absolved of personal responsibility for things that happen in my life.

It is so nice to hear that others cause all the misery in my life and that I am a victim of circumstances. But is it really so? You hear at least some of the professionals of the comfort vending variety supporting this line of thinking and saying. "Dear, dear, no one should blame you for whatever is happening. These things are not your fault. There are ways to get over these feelings. You have problems. You are not responsible for it. However, you cannot get out of it. You need help. We can help you. We would lead you to peace of mind, comfort and 'ease', you see. Ours is an efficient system to give you the good feeling you are longing for, on very favorable financial terms"

This is the enticing line extended to those in confusion, fear, guilt, anger, unforgiveness, and pain and so on by comfort-vendors. There are no two opinions about the need. There are no two opinions the technicians of the comfort-fixing variety would thrive under such needy situations and a ready, wide open market. Man needs help in getting out of the mess he finds himself in. However, if that task is converted into a profit-making business, it is bereft of all Christian understanding, compassion, morality and grace. Christian counseling has to be appreciated and evaluated in this context. "Do we love God? Do we keep his commands? The proof that we love God comes when we keep his commandments and they are not at all troublesome"[69] (I John 5,) - The Message.

PETAL-11

KNOW LOVE AND ITS VARIETIES

1. Storge –Patting, appreciating.
2. Eros- Romantic, snatching, tending to violence.
3. Philia- affection, human, bartering.
4. Pragma – Legalistic, obligated, duty-bound.
5. Ludus – playful crush, frolicking, often crossing limits
6. Mania – Obsessive, paranoid, possessive; mad love.
7. Philantia- self love, Narcissistic.
8. Agape. - Selfless, giving, divine love.

1. Storge; patting –mode-of-love.

The first basic and ordinary and simple type of love is what we call, patting love which technically is called storge; it is a simple and understandable variety. Say for example, you are watching this pen with which I am writing this note. The ink flows so freely and easily and you make out I usually enjoy the performance of the pen. You are watching this sleek black ball pen with a nice golden clip which is almost as good as a 'Waterman' pen, better than the usual 'Cross'. You casually mention; 'Alex, that is a good pen you are using, let me see it'. You take the pen in your hand and you like the feel of it. Then you scribble something on a piece of paper. You see, it is really nice. You turn back the pen to me and say "that's a good pen Alex. Very nice! I must get one like it. How much does it cost? Where is it available?"

You are taken in by the pen, normally as a courtesy at least, I should have offered it to you and said "you like it, take it, I have another one like this". I have not said that, because I didn't have another one like that, but I said "Thank you. Yes, it is a nice pen." This is patting love. You like something; you pat it and say 'good'.

At times like this, as it happened in my office, everyone has the freedom to say that they like something or the other. The matter ends there. Perhaps you may get a pen like this if you have a chance to see one like this in a shop. That is the end of the patting episode.

2. Eros, Snatching-mode-of-love

Now comes; the snatching variety of love which is termed Eros or Erotic love. One has to look at this type of love keenly and understand what it is all about. Take the case of the pen itself. You liked the pen and made an appreciative comment, but then if you snatch the pen from me and say "I want it. I am going to take it away. You get another one". You are not bothered that I am deprived of something which I need, which I am making use of. The idea is "I want; I take it, what pain it might cause you is not my problem". Your position is; "I desire, I demand, I deprive, I devour. What happens as a result of my depriving you of what you have does not bother me".

The philosophy of the Ram that jumps over a goat in the pasture is the same. I want, I get; whatever may come after it is not my responsibility. You may not like my demand. Then it is your problem. I want and I will get. This attitude lies behind all altercations, violence, scuffles, rape, killings, disputes, wars and all destruction all around the world on personal, communal, societal, national, international levels. It is all done in the name of a kind of 'love'; sheer desire, greed, coveting, gratification, lust. It may be lusting after anything others may possess. The rape of 7 years old by an 80 year old oaf, the group-rapes, the looting of the bank by robbers, dacoits, democracies wanting to turn into autocracy, border incursions and disputes, war between border states, invasion of Croatia, big finance scams, marketing of spurious drugs and merchandise of questionable quality, ill treatment of patients for more money by doctors; any act related to cheating, looting, raping, killing, arson and deliberate destruction; are all because one person/party/nation desires and decides to demand and deprive the other of what belongs to that other. Every act of evil destruction is one form or other of this external manifestation of this erotic love. This is a basic animal pattern of behavior. Even a small dispute or a disagreement in an argument can lead to senseless murder. Men bestowed with intelligence and cunning ways adopt manipulative methods to deprive others of what they desire to gratify their desires. The base of it all is desire, and at its worst form perpetrates destruction; small and big. Yet it all falls under the category of love; distorted love, bent on snatching, culminating in destruction and devastation.

3. Philia; Bartering-mode-of-love

The third variety is the Bartering love, also called Philia; the very human variety of what man understands and values as love. The principle is simple "I scratch your back and you scratch mine". None is at loss. You and I gain equally. If I give 100 rupees and expect 100 rupees worth of material or services, it is just human. Simple prostitution to bribes in offices, favors in bed rooms; every human interaction gets reduced to commercial level. I give I get, you give you get. However, the desire to get an edge in every transaction is normally in every human exchange. Bargaining in small and big ways is observable in every human intentional reaction. Look at any possible human exchange, the give and take, calculated more for better advantage by parties involved. Take any example of human interaction. Ordinarily each looks for an advantage in any exchange. So sad when this happens in bed rooms and board rooms!

Man bribes God for a better deal. Offertory boxes, hundies, paid prayers, poojas, homas, (holy rituals) prayer for healing; destroying the enemies, all are meant to bribe for a better deal from gods, touted by the priestly class, Hindu, Muslim, Christian, Sikhs, Jains, Buddhists, all worship places or business enterprises dealing out blessings for a consideration come under this broad classification.

Bribes in offices are a close offshoot of what happens in Temples, Mosques, Gurudwaras and Churches. If you want something, you must give something. Offerings in worship places are not seen and considered as bribes which are essentially legitimized bribes. We have no moral rights to complain about the bribes given to a minor god in a chair behind an office table! They regally consider and decide they need an offering. The bribing public also accepts it as a deserving offering to the deity behind the table for; there is no other way to get anything done in an office.

Would it be totally wrong to say that bartering dominates most human relationships and business interactions? Pragma in distortion (explained below) is one means, in the human sense, to get appeased or to get to be blessed. Extraction of bribe can be based on blind faiths, mutual benefits based on the give and get. One can talk interminably of the give and take philosophy which dominates most human relating. Only when one sided demand for getting more becomes aggressive, an open dispute arises leading to unpredictable troubles. What happens in the bedroom remains shrouded by and large? Small bribes are ignored as normal. Holy extortion to get more can become obsessive. Once in Kalidasa temple in Ujjain the 1960s, I had to spend almost 150 rupees to gain an entry into the inner sanctum, starting with the tolls; to take water from the temple pond, the water itself, the used and recycled garland, the incense stick and finally the entry into the temple itself. The bribes added up to a little more than 150 rupees including the free will offering back in the 1960s! Please note; my salary at that time was Rs. 275= All gods are expensive in any religion.

What is not expensive for that matter? Office clerks, retail merchants, construction lords, labor unions, teachers, priests, doctors, mendicants, goons on hire, all professionals are expensive; for ordinarily all look for a better deal in dealing with those in need. Who can or who wants to find fault or rub against the grain?

Bartering ordinarily is the human manner and system of interactions. Wives/ husbands, who do not get validated, want more and do not get all their needs met by husbands and vice versa, who do not get in quality and quantity what they desire; children who complain of the least pocket money and or unwelcome restrictions; all fall in same category and cry for more in bartering style.

4. Pragma, Logical, legalistic-mode-of-love

Pragma is considered a stable variety of love offered as a duty-bound fulfillment of an obligation and to find satisfaction in discharging dues. One does not want to be accused of not fulfilling a required duty bound 'love'. It is also considered a committed variety of long-lasting love usually found in long-term married couple who cherish companionship, enduring acceptance. Sharing and nurturing generated in a sense of 'shouldness' which can be patient and sacrificial and cannot be ignored. If participants in such enduring love relation behave contrary to the projected expectations, they stand the danger of being considered disloyal. None of the types of love are mutually exclusive. In every form of love there are areas of onerous bounds that overlap.

One example; a daughter-in-law who considers herself bound to love her mother-in-law as an obligation is under constraint to love. She wants to love her mother-in-law as her own mother but the ordinarily, perhaps avoidable rubbings create a wedge which keeps increasing the distance. But in keeping with the tradition and according to the expectations of both the individuals and their families a truce is stuck on pragmatic grounds. The absence of concerned and committed caring love she needs to offer in fulfilling the expectations vested in her; there is love of a kind that lends appearances of committed love.

5. Ludus; flirtatious-mode-of-love

Ludus refers to a type of love which can be described as; playful, flirtatious, frolicking and an infatuated variety of love that is pretty ordinarily noticeable in the early stages of romance. It could be designated as a fling, having fun and casual; uncomplicated to start with. This type of 'love', if you may call it so, can thrive if both parties who look and seek the same end, which has a built-in implicit danger of going wild in the emotional rush of romantic affectations.

As mentioned earlier no variety of love is exclusive and every type can have its expressed influence on the parties involved. Ludus stands in danger, especially of Eros having its encroaching on Ludus in ways unpredictable leading to group entertaining; to orgies and so on. This is love that needs close watching to forestall dishonorable manner of conduct; all in the enthusiasm and drive particularly of the young. It is always wise to keep a watchful eye on the possible erratic turns that this love may take. Ludus' variety of love; as we say is blind and does not see even the immediate eventualities.

6. Philantia, self, narcissistic-mode-of- love

Philantia refers to self-love, an undesirable manner of love which however is largely widespread. There is no space for others in Philantia. The individual invaded by Philantia is full of him/her and has precious little to muse about other than the self. There is nothing for anyone else, uncaring for anyone else. The individual is in love with the self, nothing far different from a narcissistic personality. The manifestations of Narcissism may not assume easily observable dimensions, but the individual remains an isolated island with no bridges to anywhere.

Any observations by anyone, positive or negative will be interpreted as lack of understanding on the part of the observer. There is no space for anyone else in the life of this individual. The term 'individual' is a considered epithet; as such people do not deserve to be addressed as 'person'. A 'person' builds bridges to others and reaches out to others in caring concern. The isolation individuals endure is interpreted and accusations leveled as uncaring others. She/he would cultivate others to buy acceptance and enjoy the glory craftily generated.

The fact is that the Philantia infested individual does not care for anyone other than the self. He is afraid of any level of disapproval; in essence being a coward and craving acceptance he might adorn himself with showy talisman and holy threads to create an impression that he is super pious and holiness on parade. They are impervious to the sensitivities of others and dismiss the extended hands in total disregard, always suspecting that others have axes to grind. Fear about individual security, suspicion of the intentions of others, makes their lives intensely uncomfortable almost reaching a paranoid fastidiousness about their appearance they dress almost gaudily to make their presence felt. Duplex strategies aimed at generating a low profile for them generate a farce and make them miserably ridiculous in turn. Understand and be accommodative of such helpless individuals.

7. Mania, possessive-mode-of- love

The very term suggests the nature of this love is almost mad in possessive love-craze.

The individual immersed in maniacal love has no other concern than possessing the object or person he craves for. Love as this individual conceives it, is for privately possessing the object for establishing authority and power over the object. Nothing short of total owning and using the object is acceptable to the manic lover. The problem with this kind of love is that the individual gripped by the desire to possess will not be deterred by any moral constraints or social barriers. It is one step ahead of the erotic blindness.

As in Eros the individual involved in such love will not easily get sobered and with ease get into violence. Proper thinking and cognition of the events precipitated by any act in mania is beyond the individual in the manic phase of love. Very close to mania is Eros; the only difference is, while Eros is a somewhat planned extension of personal aggrandizing, mania is getting by any means including causing of venomous harm. This type of love can be placed even below the animal level of erotic love. Come what may I shall possess, is the anthem of the manic lover. Thinking is not part of manic love. Though we designate this type of love as Manic 'love' there is nothing of love in it other than mad expression of a distortion of the desire for full possession of the object or person of the so called 'love'. People and objects are the same in the maniac's concept.

8. Agape, giving-mode-of-love.

The eighth type is the giving or divine love; Agape. It is separated from the caring for human variety in that Agape makes no demands. It is concerned with giving without concern for getting back in any form or any manner; giving love is the divine love exemplified by Jesus by his life and death on the Cross for mankind. Man desires love and demands and goes around in ways of extracting what is desired. Opposed to that, Agape desires nothing, demands nothing, and does not destroy anything or anyone. Agape has compassion and understanding of the needs of others. Agape sees deprivation and without being asked it endeavors to give and fulfill the needs of the needy. In this giving, the giver is not mindful of the need of the self. The highest forum of unremitted giving love!

The examples of Agape love in the human level have imperfections. Giving without any expectations and hopes of getting it back is a characteristic of Agape. Unconditional giving as it is has limitations on the human level. Agape as it qualifies as unconditional without expecting back anything at all is totally divine. Man succeeds in this type of giving by adopting the pattern of giving practiced and demonstrated by Jesus and saints of old during the time of their earthly ministry. From the conversion of water to wine in Cana, to the restoring of the ear of the Chief Priest's soldiers, was given with no ties attached.

His acts were limited. He accepted what was offered in love. He ate food from Martha and Maria's house, accepted hospitality at Zacchaeus' place, partook in feasts in Simon's place, was thankful for the anointing of His head with perfume by Mary

He said "Foxes have holes, birds of the air have nests but the son of Man has no place to lay His head". Lk.9:58. (NIV) Whatever he possessed, he gave away freely. His possessions were blessings, feeding and healing. He didn't go hungry, except for the 40 days of fasting, prior to His testing by the devil. All kinds of comforts were offered to Him; He refused and rebuked the tempter.

His giving culminated in the giving of himself on the cross, shedding of his own blood in an eternal covenant relationship with mankind. Such giving is unusual, almost impractical by human standards. Yet His beloved disciple John said and again kept saying that the Lord and Master gave himself in serving us and we also ought to follow his example and give likewise. Easily said than done! Yet all His disciples sacrificed their lives in setting examples of giving. He made it easy for

His disciples by offering a place for them to be; that was his own body. The invitation was explicit which amounted to "Come and abide in me, abide in my word, abide in my love. Then you will be able to get all your needs met and have all things in abundance to give".[70] (John.15)

His giving was not in materials only. The two things He asked of His disciples were, love others as He loves and serve others as He serves; to the point of washing the feet of the lowly. Such giving and serving is the characteristic of Agape. Ordinarily, man is afraid and ill-equipped for such giving and serving. Yet, He assured us we can do greater things than He did while with us.[71] (John.14: 12). The one extra item He gave to all indiscriminately was 'forgiveness'. Without forgiveness, there can be no disposition to give even to the unlovable as He evidenced in giving. The first thing He offered to his tormentors was forgiveness. That forgiveness qualified Him for resurrection on the third day.

Forgiveness is a precondition to resurrection and new life. This new life prompts to give without expectation. Teaching in Agape is giving away what we receive in free divine filling. That is the standard of love prescribed and expected of all those who follow Christ. This wide loving is made possible or impossible as it may seem, in fair thinking or unfair thinking, depending on the personal faith and realized spiritual measure of the thinker.

PETAL-12

PRAYER AND BELONGING

Many years back in Africa after I talked to a group on aspects of "Spiritual Maturity" a very bright young person came up to me and said, "Prayer to me is almost worthless. I spend time talking to God. It appears to me my prayers are failing on deaf ears. But I go through the motions because my elders expect me to". "Prayers fall on deaf ears" is a typical feeling when we assume God is a person with ears and eyes. We want to limit God to man-size which is technically termed as "Anthropomorphizing" of God. It has many advantages for thinking men. A god conceived in thinking and contained by emotions, localized and accessible is a physical incongruence. That god is accessible even if that god does not rise up to expectations most of the time. A thinking man does not have any alternatives as he does not care or have the disposition to "see" beyond his thinking to establish an identity for his god. So whatever is perceived and seems to have listening ears is more likely to be accepted as an answer to the search for such a god really does not amount to even a substitute god.

I tried to tell the young man, prayer is not some exercise to influence God and get our agenda accepted. It is, on the contrary, a submission to be influenced and guided by God according to our belief system. He had a hard time assimilating the concept for he has not dealt with prayer in that sense at all. He was smart enough to reject men, women and material gods, yet a personal, giving, loving, supporting comforting god of his specification was hard for him to conceptualize. He wanted to be close, yet distant to a disciplining God whom he hesitated to witness in public.

The young man's god appeared to be a secret god. He said he always prayed in the secrecy of his bedroom as the Bible instructs: "But when you pray, go into your room, close the door and pray to your Father, who is unseen. Then, your Father, who sees what is done in secret, will reward you. And when you pray, do not keep or babbling like pagans, for they think they will be heard because of their many words"[72] Matt. 6: 6-7.

The young man insisted that he never babbled as babbling goes. "But I kept telling God what my needs were and how I expected to be rewarded for the time I spent with god. Am I not right in expecting a reply for my supplications or applications or whatever? Even government offices do that!" The obvious mistake of trying to catch the ears of God through demanding and moving Him to do things the way we need, according to our time-table is a defeating strategy because of the wrong concept we produce of God within ourselves and because of the wrong expectations we foster.

God is open to our reach when we are available for Him to have space within us for Him. Prayer and movements resembling prayer may take place in any form anywhere but for meaningful communication from God, man has to be open to receive. For the purpose of receiving the receptacle has to be free of all accumulated muck. A cleansed receptacle free of all complaints and filled with gratitude is a prerequisite to receive anything at all from the Holy God.

The secret to receive from God whatever reward one expects is that transparent purity within which resonate to God's love in commitment. Make space for God within. That as you understand now; the very first requirement is to empty ourselves of erring concept of God and. God rewards openly but our destinies are shaped and determined by the way we respond to Him and His giving in love.

What is said above does not take away the importance and significance of public, corporate prayer. There never was nor is a lonely Christian. Christians belong and every Christian has to conform to this community formation which is implicit in the institution of Christianity as branches of the same True Vine. Together in Him, Christians form the body of Christ and together they flourish accepting and taking on the responsibility for each other. Their very presence together communicates the quality of their participation in prayer as one body. Larger incredible and limitless results are achieved in the body in private and corporate public prayer by being and belonging together and responding to God in His love, making space for God in our lives. Existing realities may cause confusions. Elaborating on that could be inelegant.

The strength of the Christian is his belonging and that makes him indebted to others who together belong to the Body.

Reaching help to another branch in stress and need belonging to the True Vine is a given and accepted responsibility. There is nothing out of the ordinary in that act. It is expected of an abiding Christian, which means every Christian has to act as a means to bless others in the Body and outside. No one can opt out in indifference which will amount to denying the Body itself. No normal Christian can do it; no Christian counselor would do that. Counseling as comforting, sharing, building up, teaching, encouraging, praying for all; are normal happenings in a Christ-centered relationship in His body as we all belong to Him and have our being in Him.

We belong and are one in Him.

PETAL-13

WITH GENTLENESS

"Let your gentleness be evident to all", said Paul in[73] Philippians 4:5. Peter refers to "the unfading beauty of a gentle and quiet spirit, which is of great worth in God's sight"[74] 1 Pet. 3:4.

Gentleness is a great attribute of a Christian, an essential attitude in a Christian Counselor. But we miss gentleness and tend to lose our essential humility when things go wrong and against our expectations.

When others turn unappreciative and people around us appear hostile, it becomes hard to keep a gentle interior. When our striving turns futile and when we notice others are causing us hindrances, we feel convinced we are failing despite hard work. That brings up all that is not gentle in us. When we know that no one really cares about what happens to us and in all our lives we have gathered only rejection; gentleness gives way to bitterness. And at times we begin to believe that God himself has forsaken us and the very ground under us seems to sink; there is no room for any noble gentleness in us. We arrive at a point where nothing makes a difference and we shout "to heck with it" and reach for the bottle or turn hostile to all, knowing we are done! At these times where do we look for strength to stand up and have a sense of calm assurance?

There was a time when I used to say endurance is the thing and it is sheer dogged hard work. Work, work, work up and be worn out and there rewards are bound to happen. My professors told me there is nothing that will replace hard work and that is not a lie. On the first day on the parade ground in April 1962, as an officer cadet in the National Cadet Corps, my company commander Captain Ghatge shouted at me, "Hey, Mathew, you are marching like a pregnant duck". I think I marched almost a month that first day. That night my body and legs ache to the point that I couldn't sit in any position.

Four years later at the end of a refresher course I was declared the Second Best Officer. Ask me again, did I gain any gentleness after the officers' training course? Yes! I gained a commendation, recognition, a promotion as a group commander leading four NCC companies in the area, but not gentleness of any kind. In the bargain I lost whatever humanity that was left in my brain, gentleness was a far cry in the officer that was stuffed in me. My job was to produce patriots who would be ready to take up arms, if and when the need arrived. My vocabulary on the parade ground at that time was studded and it stank all the way home too. From there I traveled far to become a Christian counselor.

I want to tell you, production lines for producing proficient officers are not particularly endowed with gentleness. Serious, no-nonsense producers push for production with fierce efficiency employing monster techniques geared to greater output. The mechanics too have the same objective before them. Production calls for calculation about input and output, balancing both sides of an equation with more balance on the output side. There is no room for gentleness there.

Counselors may enter into counseling practice with a production line philosophy goading them from within: "I must produce better and noticeable results".

"The people I subject to therapy should evidence positive improvement. I must use modern methodology, mod-vocabulary and efficient tools to produce an impressive reputation. The consumer is my concern and that is why I even call it 'client-centered-therapy'. Efficiency is the issue. I must act in affability, classical acceptance, positive regard with decorum, high-level advanced empathy using all the latest tools in the industry to evoke positive changes". These are understandable, ambitious, balanced counselor positions!

But then what we are looking at here is the role of gentleness in a Christian who chooses to be a counselor. It is understood and a written code in counseling that a counselor needs to offer unconditional acceptance to the counselee. While that is a paramount counseling principle, it is equally if not massively important; that the counselor must find acceptance in the mind of the counselee, if there is to be anything positive happening in any counseling of any description. This position would invite a question, "Why on earth should a counselee unconditionally accept a counselor especially before the process takes off?"

Ordinarily, the counselor observes and attends to the counselee in total acceptance because of professional compulsions. The counselee has no such finesse to contribute to. An air-hostess-like studied plastic smile does not go far enough to warrant an unconditional acceptance. What would the counselee find in the eyes, facial musculature, body postures and gestures of the counselor beyond the studied standardized drill in the counseling room? The studied gentleness of a smooth operative does not go very far in convincing the counselee of the essential goodness and the gentleness of the person. Please remember that the counselee is assessing you during the process. What is the picture you are offering to the counselee? Are you seen as a benevolent presence by the counselee?

"Let your gentleness be evident to all". That gentleness comes from within, not because we regurgitate it from our guts, but because of the gentle spirit of Christ that dwells within. The Christian counselor has to open his heart to the Christ who waits to abide in Him and evidence his gentles in his very being as an abiding branch at peace in abiding and producing the fruit of gentleness. We shall produce much fruits as we abide in Him, gentle, kind, patient, sweet and humble.

Shouldn't it be so! Some seventy years back my father told me this story, acting it out with aplomb.

He usually did this sort of thing to make a point. As a teenager I was keen on going to places and I wanted to go to an old church some twenty miles away from home. The way to that place was mainly by the banks of the Achankovil River and I always loved the walk by this river with three or four ferries in between. He was concerned about me getting blisters in the sole of my feet. So, he suggested we go by boat. I knew that was going to take time and I said, "it is not twenty miles, it must be much less".

He laughed aloud uncharacteristically and told me this story about a venerable old man in our neighborhood who had a way of making others say what he wanted to hear. I knew this man. When I was younger I was afraid of him like other children in the village. He had an imposing figure with a bushy curled up mustache and always went about with a sturdy and flashy walking stick. His mouth was blood red with chewing of pan and tobacco which he would spit out expertly in an evil jet without care to where he was positioned. He would roll up his dhoti to inelegant heights above his sizable butt and let his "Kerala tie" hang out behind as the tail of a rambling lion. He was a sort of minor feudal loudmouth who was definitely not liked by us children. My father knew what regard the children of the village had for this man and yet he chose this particular man to drive a lesson to me.

In those days there were no public transports to speak of. Mostly people walked any reasonable distance with ease. Ten to twenty miles were within usual walking distances. This old man was walking to a neighboring village and on the way he met a traveler and asked him how far the particular village he was going to. "It is about eight miles sir", said the traveler. "Is it that far?" the old man remarked with some degree of annoyance in his tone. A bit taken aback at the tone, the traveler added, "It is actually eight miles sir, but if you think it is less, it should be so sir". The old man walked on without saying anything further but somewhat less annoyed.

He emitted a narrow red jet with added force and twirling his stick. The old man reached the village. After he was received by the village chief and feted as an honorable guest, he got ready to leave. As he was about to leave he asked his host,

"Actually how far is my village from here?' The chief did not take any time to respond. He said, "It must be eight miles to where your temple stands". He had no doubt about the distance. "Is it that far?" asked the old man with a certain disapproval of the distance mentioned. The chief sensed the displeasure and hastened to add, "Actually, I think it is eight miles, but if you think it is less, it is indeed lesser than that sir". "I thought so", said the old man with some degree of satisfaction and walked off happily twirling his stick.

The narration may appear funny but I got the message alright. Today the message comes back with added meaning. The fact is people want to hear what they want to hear. If you tell people what they want to hear, they are pleased. You can fool a lot of people by telling them what they love to hear with some pleasantly interlaced calculated garnishing with subtle or even gross flattery. A con art is a great cheap art of fooling the gullible. Soothsayers, astrologers, hand and face readers, omen interpreters, god-men and women, hypnotists, 'Pranic' healers, some shallow faith healers and their ilk have perfected the art of sensitively smothering people with what they would want to hear. It is an unfailingly huge, crude and cheap con business principle.

One glaring example: Children are told convincingly in the presence of all their friends that their under-performance is not their fault. It is because they are pestered by their mothers or fathers to study and study. It is also because they are unhealthily compared with others. The acceptance you get is performance based. Naturally you fall back on your performance. Take it easy. It is not your fault. Relax, do everything at your own pace. Go to the books when you feel you are ready to study. The children love to hear it and are happy to follow the expert advice. Teachers are obliquely happy that the parents are the scapegoats.

It is true, relaxed learning is the best way to learn. But that principle need not be ingested putting the anxious parents in the dock. Are there no ways to help anxious parents and stressed children other than creating scapegoats of the parents?

Making the children aware of their responsibilities and helping them to grow up through healthy habits of learning and hard work are likely to be shunned by young children. Making someone else responsible for their lack of hard work is a welcome strategy for the children.

The damage to the family is not a problem for the experts. Their focus is the fee they collect from the parents who pay to make learned enemies of their own children. The art is a perfected one. Tell the children what they want to hear and make their parents pay for the lies! Does that also come under the province of counseling? Should it?

PETAL-14

THE PATH TO BLESSINGS

John chapter 13 deals about the path to blessings.

[75] John.13:12, "Do you understand what I have done for you?" 13:15: "I have set you an example that you should do as I have done for you" 13:17: "Now that you know these things, you will be blessed if you do them".

These three statements were addressed to the disciples by Jesus soon after the "washing of feet" in the Upper Room; the night before He was crucified. Apart from instituting what evolved into the Sacrament of Holy communion Jesus had a specific purpose of setting an example for his disciples. What He wanted them to understand and practice was unambiguously given to them. It simply meant, if you want to be blessed you must do as I did in all humility.

Later in the same chapter he gave his disciples "one new commandment" in verse 34 and asking us to follow it up. The importance He attached to these; One Commandment and One Example should not be lost on the Christian counselor.

A Christian counselor is expected to give up on any special status to which he might think he is entitled. The Lord washed the feet of the disciples after making it clear to all present in that room that He does not stand on protocol.[76] John 13: 3-5 makes the picture even clearer. He knew who He was and He knew what he was about to do. A person who is not fully aware of who he is, will never be bold enough to bend his knees before a lesser person according to our social standards. Jesus brought himself down to the level of a servant proving what He said in[77] Matthew 20:28: "Just as the son of Man did not come to be served, but to serve, and to give his life as ransom for many".

The Christian counselor has to take this object example lesson very seriously. His calling is to serve and that service has to be done internalizing the principle behind this example. Humility in its most elegant form is discernible in this example. Jesus accepted His disciples as friends and went a step further to elevate them even above that status. He literally turned a servant and washed their feet. And He says to us 'you will be blessed if you do these things'. St. Paul drives the point home when he says, "Be devoted to one another in brotherly love. Honor one another above yourselves".[78] Rom. 12:10).

The Christian counselor should know "these things" and do "these things" in the very spirit of the matter as Jesus intended; to receive blessings. Without that, the counselor would miss the blessings and would fail to bless others through his counseling, because he thinks he can pull it off by himself.

Let us look at some of the manner of things that go on right around us. The ruler of a great nation, Vladimir Putin stands ready to erase a whole nation of Ukraine.

Is it by any chance due to global compulsions of a drive for prosperity or because of his greed for the land of Croatia?

Sri Lanka this time is burning itself down without the help of Hanumanji. They do not want that to happen, but all the same they are doing just that. China is poised for global economic autonomy not because they are ardently eager to lift the global economy. Pakistan and India are facing each other in hair-trigger hostility. Iranian religious bosses have no qualms about shooting down women who refuse to wear a headscarf.

Closer home, a 14 year old girl; Nirbhaya is brutally gang raped in a bus and left to die in inhuman deprived animal arrogance of racial supremacy? A seven year old girl is raped by her own father. A mother forcefully gifts her daughter for prostitution. Gang rapes are more common than summer rains. A political party drives away a thriving industry to a neighboring state, because of an assumed superiority over other political parties, leaving hundreds jobless.

Eating place serves rancid decayed food to unsuspecting customers. Spurious drugs are manufactured and sold to sick people with no concerns for the enormous fatal consequences. Religious leaders turn comfort-vendors, doing untold harm to unsuspecting believers and collecting financial benefits on top of it.

Bribing right, left and center is the norm of the day if you want anything at all done in any Government office and even more in village offices.

Goons thrive selling narcotics, bootlegging and doing open killing business as it were, right under the very nose; before the eyes of conniving officer lords.

Rich killers and rapists go about in gleeful abandon fooling the public and judiciary in never ending drama with the help of smart advocates who have no hesitations to dance for money, knowing full well that even kites do not fly over money. Negotiable law-enforcement agents accept hush money even on the roadside for petty or huge traffic offenses.

Efforts go on in fast tract in the full knowledge of all concerned to sell off even profitable public undertakings to private sharks with financial clout and right connections. Denuding forest cover thus weakening ecologically fragile environments, sand mining and quarrying delicately balanced environmentally precarious regions, clearly seeing imminently obvious disaster in the foreseeable nearer future. Defaming and spreading false information about honorable people to edge them out from public visibility is colored in elegance in politics.

All sorts of imaginable and unimaginable things keep happening all around us. We keep wondering what the heck! But keep wondering and wanting to do something about it, if possible, knowing full well, nothing is possible when the fence start eating the crop. A Counselor of whatever shade must make it a point not to be dragged aside to deflect from his chosen path of loving service.

PETAL-15

BEING ALERT

A practice that will go a long way in equipping the Christian counselor to "speak the right word in season" is to spend regular and a set time with the Lord God, preferably early in the morning when distractions are likely to be minimal. By being with God every morning the counselor learns the art to listen to the Lord. He speaks in gentle whispers and it is not easy to hear what he says if we are lost in the static of everyday rush.

We need to choose a quiet time and be silent before the Lord. "Be silent and know that I am God"[78] Ps. 46: 10 are God's words which do communicate to us the intention behind it. Knowing God develops an "in-touch" contact with the Master who is ready to communicate.

God takes a position in which He lets those who really want to see; to really see fully and He makes those who really want to hear to hear fully. He is aware of the touch of those who really want to touch even the hem of His garment. The Christian counselor needs to be intensely aware of these facts to be "in-touch" with Jesus. If you want to speak what the Spirit lets you, learn to listen more to the Spirit.

Listen more and learn to listen more intently. If anyone wants to write, one has to read much more. If anyone wants to counsel, take counsel from the true counselor, the Holy Spirit. We need to know that God intends to teach all counselors representing Him to be alert to His voice. We need to pray without ceasing and that means our spiritual antennae need to be uncoiled and raised up to catch every quiver of the Holy Spirit and our sensitivities raised to be receptive to every gentle whisper of the Spirit. Being silent and being receptive is not the end in itself, but the means to be in touch and be filled with His Word on offer.

Having received the "right Word in season", obedience is the next important step. In all humility we need to remember that God is unlikely to show us something if He knows that we would not heed and do it any old way! When we begin the act of obedience there is further revelation. By the same standard when we refuse to obey, God will stop communicating with us. Our God is not complicated. He expects obedience as he opens up to us in privileged communication in the silence of our hearts.

It is that simple.

Does it appear complicated?

Being in touch with Jesus brings in that extra dimension that is needed in ministering His presence, feeble as it may be, to those in any kind of need. The fact remains that the Christian counselor ministers the love, peace and joy of the Lord Jesus and for that, being in touch with Jesus is important; by that I mean enjoy an abiding relation with Jesus which He freely offers. Listen to hear, look to see, reach out to touch are some basics in filling our being with God and His blessings. The essence of being a blessing, as a counselor in Him knows, is to be blessed to bless.

Counselor's need to know and 'See'.

"My purpose is that they may be encouraged in heart and united in love, so that they may have the full riches of complete understanding, in order that they may know the mystery of God, namely Christ, in whom are hidden all the treasures of wisdom and knowledge"[79] (Col. 2: 2-3).

Christian counseling demands wisdom and knowledge rooted in faith. A Christian counselor should have the full riches of complete understanding. Christian counseling should be open to the mystery of God, namely Christ. The minimum inference that follows this observation is that counseling is not an easy task to be taken lightly or casually. Without knowledge, understanding, wisdom and an awareness of the mystery of Jesus Christ, counseling in His name and on His behalf will not happen. On the contrary awareness of the mystery of Jesus Christ creates a new sensibility for seeing, a new way of perceiving, and a new pattern of observing, reasoning, choosing and presenting

Christian counseling cannot be likened to changing a flat tire. With practically no shift in procedure you and I can do the changing with the same expected results.

Say; you have a flat tire. As soon as you notice it, curse the road in a somewhat audible voice. Give a big kick to the flat tire. Make sure at least some passersby are benefited by your grit. If your wife is in the car, it is standard procedure to shout at her to pull the boot lever. Then open the boot. Cursing may continue at this point too. Take the spare tire, tool kit and jack out from the boot. Put a stopper behind one or two of the other wheels. Test whether the spare tire has enough pressure. Take out the wheel cap off the flat tire. Lightly loosen the nuts. Jack up the vehicle. Take out the nuts. Remove the flat tire.

There is room for a loud one here. Put the spare on to the wheel drum. Tighten the nuts. Lower the jack. Tighten the nuts further and see it is properly tight. Fix the wheel cap back. Put the flat tire and the jack back in the boot. You may curse the person who spreads nails on the road. Wipe your hands on some rag. That is one more apt occasion to shout at your wife for not keeping some tissues around. Grouch and ride on. Drop the tire at the fuel station for repair.

The procedure is standard. You and I get standard results as expected. You can seriously improve the results if you give another whooping kick to the side of the wheel before you even kneel down to deal with it. It takes away your attention to your hurting leg and the tire would then heave a satisfied sigh. Then on, the job would go on with less standard screaming.

Christian counseling is slightly different, I am afraid. There is no standard procedure because we do not deal with standard samples. The Lord God has made each one of us as unique persons. If I develop patterns to deal with persons as I feel right and teach you the same line of approach would that bring out the same type of results? Assuming that I have perfected a system and you learned it as I practice it, would you produce the same set of results even if you practice it on a person with similar conditions as I worked on? Counseling as psychology has no predictability. Counseling is not like fixing a spare wheel. Counseling is not a science per se. Psychology has never been even an empirical science with no predictability or repeatability. Starting with Freud it stood solidly as personal opinions to date.

The fact is you are unique, I am unique, the person you work with is unique, and everyone else is unique. Systems produced through usually slanted personal opinions are not in any way suitable to be accepted as standardized models for dealing with unique individuals.

It is a sobering humbling bit of truth.

Everyone with some personal piece of esoteric knowledge would display it as the universal principle worth emulating by all else. Perfectly understandable as basic human deviation! But we do not have to take such deviations seriously. We have done that mistake time and time over forgetting or forsaking the very clear exhortation; "See to it that no one takes you captive through hollow and deceptive philosophy, which depends on human tradition and the basic principles of this world rather than on Christ"[80] (Col. 2:8).

All the uniqueness of all people is known to the Creator of all people. We all are his handiwork. What I am trying to say is simply to follow His directions in dealing with his creation.

Let me repeat the verse I recorded in the beginning of this article: My purpose is that we may be encouraged in heart and united in love, so that they may have the full riches of complete understanding, in order that they may know the mystery of God, namely Christ, in whom are hidden all the treasures of wisdom and knowledge[81] (Col. 2: 2-3)

All that is said in this chapter deals with the standard manner of counseling including the Christian varieties.

Counseling simply cannot be standardized.

PETAL-16

PURPOSE AND PRIORITY

Christ in you is the hope of glory[82] (Col. 1:27). God has endowed us with senses. Through our body functions and the senses, we stay in contact with our environment. We interact with others through our intelligence and emotions, both part of what we understand as our mind. We make choices with our volition (will). We commune with God through our Spirit. All the three are interactive and are part of the whole organism that is man.

The Lord God who is Omnipresent is experientially palpable in our surroundings if we are fine-tuned to his presence in all the aspects of our personality; that is to say in the body, mind and spirit. He is around everywhere all the time. He is a pulsating entity simultaneously present at all places if he can be believed in his own words, "Lo I am with you always, even to the end of the age"[83] (Matt.28: 20b, NASB).

Who can refute that promise unless one denies his deity? The only thesis as Francis Schaeffer puts it is: 'God IS'. Everything else is because God IS. Our lack of awareness does not alter the fact of the Omni-active God's omnipresence, omniscience, and omnipotence. The simple fact is: God IS present here, within and without us right now, everywhere, every time. In the making of a counselor there are many things that happen which have no logical or scientific defense. It may mean nothing to some people. The transformation of such events brought in me was overwhelming, bringing in a kind of quality in my counseling which defies all logic to this day.

Meditate on the last part of[84] John 14:19[b] which says, "BECAUSE I live, you will also live". As I meditated on this slice of a verse in the seventies for over five years, practically on every Friday I became increasingly convinced. There is nothing in me per se, as a counselor which brought blessings to the people who came to me for counseling.

Our gross insensitivity to the total Lordship of Jesus and His all-pervading authority tend to discount the reality of His willingness to commune with us moment by moment. He has extended a standing invitation to us to abide in His Word, abide in His Love and simply abide in Him. The Lord himself has categorically promised He will abide in us if we will receive Him into ourselves. Meditation is a 'metaconscious' effort to sense the Lord Jesus within and experience our abiding in Him. Meditation is a fine-tuning to savor the abiding relationship that works. Our lack of awareness of Jesus and His nearness to us seriously impedes us in effective, affirmative and wholesome living. In the absence of such a Spirit-filled fullness, we would feel empty and lacking substance and purpose. That is when we go hunting for experiences that would give us satiation in things of the world. We have no guarantee that we would succeed in gaining gratification in things and people we desire. We come to accept the fact that things and people betray and fail us, never catching up to our expectations. The obvious outcomes in such situations lead to defeat and a 'victim' mind-set. So we think and we are cheated from gaining what we desire.

On the contrary a pulsating awareness of Jesus in us breaks through the private inner barriers we have set for ourselves and give us an intense sense of belonging to him. Our realization begins to have a physical reality about it when our body also senses Jesus in and about us.[85] Revelation 3:21, is specific assurance on this.

Human awareness is not limited to the intellectual, emotional or spiritual areas only. If awareness is bereft of the physical dimension, it ceases to have wholesomeness about it as an experience. That Jesus is the life of a believer is not to be compartmentalized and dumped in an intellectual or emotional or spiritual corner of his awareness to be brushed up and dealt with only when he engages himself in ritualistic prayer or spiritual activities. Christ fills the whole being of a believer. Every touch, every word, every act and non-act of the believer is to be, by and through and in Jesus, for, apart from Him, we can do nothing.[86] (John.15:5)

Christian meditation is for elevating the consciousness of the believer to this level of an experiential reality. This was the experience of great men and women of God, beautifully exemplified in the life of David, the man after the heart of God. Do not dismiss this as 'work' as some people would argue, because it is not, it is grace in operation. Christian meditation is not anything difficult or esoteric. There is no hard and fast rule or regulated physical drills associated with it. Please do not think it is some 'work to gain' the kingdom. However there are some general guidelines, which will make the meditation more enjoyable and prevent physical discomfort due to posture.

A convenient time, preferably the morning time as we begin our day is most congenial for meditation. If you have the trust and humility to say along with David, "I trust in Thee O Lord, I say, 'Thou art my God' my times are in Thy hand"[87] (Ps. 31:14, 15), then you have the courage to abandon yourself in His care.

Wherever we go 'Thou art there'[88] (Ps. 139:8b); wherever I am I can 'pour out my heart before Him'[89] Ps. 62:3b); I can remain still and know that He is God[90] (Ps. 46:10). Then I can act on His invitation to go to Him and give all my burdens and heavy loads. "Come to Me all you who labor and are heavily burdened and I will give you rest"[91] (Matt. 11:28).

A slight digression is called for here. We all want to unburden ourselves. What exactly are our burdens? Where and how do we carry burdens? How can we get rid of our burdens? We receive information through our senses. Destination of all information is the brain. They travel as electrical impulses in nerves and end up as chemicals in the neurons. Though these chemicals are stored in our neurons, the neuro-secretions, in a matter of seconds, get defused to all living cells of the body. This is very unlike food, water and air that we take into our system. What is not needed in the body is excreted. Food, water (apart from some metabolic water) and air do not increase in measure once within the body. However, this is not the case with thoughts. Thoughts are multiplied by more thoughts which increase the sheer volume of the original thought and they pervade every cell and subcellular parts of the whole organism.

Happy thoughts get shared and celebrated. Sad thoughts are uncontrollably multiplied and if not shred, get stored as heavy burdens. We need to realize the Lord Jesus is referring to this stored up burden which breaks people. We need to go to him with these burdens. He says, "…..I will give you rest". This is the 'rest' we stand in need of! Let us look at the ways to go about dumping the burden and gain rest in the process. This is an integral part of what we refer as the Life of Abiding. Abiding calls for rest and implies rest in the experiential and existential sense. A heart not at rest has no rest in itself to offer. A Christian counselor has to receive the rest that Christ offers to share with those in need of rest. An abiding Christian-meta-love-counselor transcends to be a conveyor-belt for the rest Christ offers.

Physical Relaxation

The body must cease from work. There are only two types of work that our body can perform. These are the contraction of muscles and secretion from glands.

Complete stoppage of muscle contraction and cessation of secretion happen only in a dead body. We only consider reduction of these functions to the minimal possible tone level within a living body. We should spend some time learning the process of physical relaxation.

Since the body is capable of only two types of work, contraction of the muscles and secretion from the glands, we can learn to relax by loosening our voluntary muscles. The body would sense this relaxation, send up the information to the brain, and produce a calming effect in the body. Depending on the richness of the relaxation of the voluntary muscles, the involuntary muscles too will tend to relax allowing the thoracic and abdominal organs too to relax. As quality of the relaxation deepens, the glands also would ease up and would discharge less, causing the organism as a whole to be less tense and more relaxed.

Pouring Out inner contents of 'Heart/Mind'

The next step in relaxation is spreading this relaxed state into the area of the soul or mind. As we gain physical relaxation, the relaxed state of the body must be supported by the mind. And where is the mind? Some would say it is in the brain, some would suggest the hypothetically conceived 'heart'. We all know there is no such localized 'heart' performing the functions of the mind. The truth is that every cell in the body or the whole body functions as the mind. That calls for deep relaxation. So, when we indicate relaxation of the mind, we mean the relaxation of the whole organism, all the systems of the body, all the organs, organelles, cells and sub-cellular particles. If not tension would be produced anew by fresh stressful thinking and added burden. A relaxed posture and regulated breathing will reduce physical discomfort. The moment breathing is mentioned holy antennae will go up and harp: "Oh, this is work, totally unchristian". While ignorance is not an acceptable plea, there is no point in countering that point of view. Look at the facts as they are and be satisfied about the simple reality and the ultimate truth about the matter.

One basic and easy way to spread relaxation all over is to bring the 'mind' also at rest; not converging the thoughts on any concerns and stress of any sort. In other words empty the total mental content. A simple method is to focus the thoughts on nothing and give up all efforts to think but ease into experiencing the total absence of thoughts but only an experience of nothingness or emptiness in the present moment.

Some early efforts can include focusing attention on a verse or even a word from the verse that connotes a needed blessing or a quality. Go over it in mind bringing to conscious mind the divine intent and purpose for you behind that Verse/Word. For example every morning dawns with new possibilities and words such as: Peace, Love, Joy, Tolerance, Self-control, Abundance, Calmness, Acceptance, Patience, Goodness, Kindness, Faithfulness, Humility, Gratitude, Contentment, Wholeness, Energy, Forgiveness, Expectancy, Blessedness, and ever so many wonderful blessing words and/or authentic verses to substantiate it.

Let me assist you in easing into awareness of the Lord filling your whole being. Take this simple experience. Open your eyes and look around the room you are in now and take notice of all things that you see present in the room. Notice all the objects you see.

Now slowly close your eyes and try to 'SEE' around you. You see only darkness with some splotches of pinkish red. You do not SEE any objects as such.

Open your eyes slowly again and look. You see all the objects which were there earlier. You see nothing more. You saw nothing when your eyes were closed.

Consider and understand the depth of the following terms which we employ to know God 'the Omnipresent, Omnipotent, Omniactive, Omnimorphic, Omniscient, Omni Benedictio, Omnipresence of the Omni-Omni God'; who is all around and within us.

When the eyes were open and when the eyes were shut you did not see the Omnipresent God. Seeing is only one of the senses. We can see, hear, taste, smell or touch to 'sense' an object. But the dimensions of our senses have to expand to totally SENSE God wherever we are beyond the senses as we normally experience it. We call this the sixth sense or in Sanskrit lingo as the Atheendriya ngyan *(awareness beyond senses)*. A Christian-meta-love-counselor in his meta-cognition becomes aware of His presence all around and within. It is only in that state the Omniactive, Omniscient, Omnipotent, and Omnibenedictio, Omnimorphic, Omnipresent, Omni-Omni, Lord can use the humble loving meta-love-counselor for His healing purposes.

Learning the art of giving up tension-producing thoughts onto the Lord who stands ready before you to receive all your burdens is not hard. It is simply a trusting step in faith you need to take. Pour out your heart to him[92] (Ps. 62:8) and then find rest as it says in the same[93] Psalm 62:1. My soul finds rest in God alone. We find rest is in the shedding of all heart/mental content by handing it off and handing it over to Jesus who accepts it and gives rest in body, mind and spirit, in its stead. That would be ideal state-of-being in the world as a meta-love-counselor, existentially and holistically speaking. Just a reminder, the impact of[94] (Mat. 11:28) should not be lost on you. The brain catches on with the rested, relaxed state reducing the pituitary activity which in turn relaxes all internal organs and cells.

It is well that the Meta-love-counselor takes note of the fact that as you ministers to the need of the person sitting before you, please remember that the counselee is watching you and drawing inferences about you from what is visibly noticeable. The counselee is sensitive to all little expressions and what it coveys. Your tone and inflections, facial expressions, body movements, thoughtless gesticulations, even the mode of dressing, your peace or lack of it are blotted in. Take care to be at perfect peace with the Lord, within yourself and with the person in front of you. Even the smallest change in voice, expressions in the eyes, gives away where you are in terms of oneness with the peace and joy of the Lord. Let there be nothing in your dispositions that would cause a doubt about your purity and integrity. You are meant to be holy and pure in the filling of the Spirit in you. There should be no hesitance whatsoever in being you as you are in His Grace. You are not in a show business putting up appearances, you must be transparent as glass, and you have nothing to hide. What the counselee should see in you is, at least a feeble reflection of the abounding grace of the Lord Jesus.

PETAL-17

NEED TO DEFINE CHRSTIAN COUNSELING

Note: (Counseling /Guidance, Counselor /Guide are used interchangeably)

This is a rather large chapter. I would caution you to read this chapter in four or five turns!)

Guidance-Counseling as such has become a household term in the urban areas of our country. It is widely spread even in rural areas of the South. Amidst the Christian population all over India, counseling is accepted as a socio-religious activity sanctioned and encouraged by the church. Within or without; we meet different kinds of attitudes in Christian counselors towards this ministry. I prefer to qualify counseling as a ministry because it is in all reality ministering Christian love in practical terms, leading to total healing and wholeness. However, at least five different types of counselors are identifiable:

First type engages in counseling for whatever personal gain they might derive from it.

The second type firmly believes they are entitled to be counselors by virtue of their credentials.

A third group believes that they have special gifts of 'seeing' and are therefore equipped to be counselors.

The fourth group is constrained by the love that gives itself to comfort those who are in any trouble.

The fifth group has their focus on Jesus in meta-love-counseling

In other words, we may see the five groups this way:

1. Counseling for personal gains.
2. Counseling in presumptive authority.
3. Counseling in assumed special personal powers.
4. Counseling in and because of the love that constraints.
5. Counseling focuses on Jesus in their counseling.

In the mainline churches, mostly the clergy practiced it until the recent past, perhaps not termed as counseling as such. Organized service setups practice on secular and psychological counseling lines.

We will leave that aside in the context of this book. Every counselor has the freedom to counsel as she/he understands counseling. Every artist has the freedom and right to express and practice their art, every seller to sell his wares. Whether the art or any product on sale are for the express purpose of helping those who would buy and use it is a·mute question, and we need not spend time on its ethical moral aspects. It would serve no possible positive ends. Psychological/secular counseling modules practiced widely are functional tools to disburse the comfort that assures freedom from 'dis-ease'. What does a person volunteering himself/herself for getting counseled expect to experience? The list of expectations can extend ad infinitum in proportion to the number of persons in need. This will be roughly equivalent to the total population of people in pain and needs on earth. An effort at a largely limited generalization only is possible here.

Let us first consider what all comes under the ambit of counseling. The list and the understanding of the process could be infinitely variable and tediously large. But in asking some questions, we get a glimpse of the endless aspects of this ministry we understand as counseling. There may be some obvious repetitions and some inadvertent and unintentional omissions too.

Articulating a better grip on Christian counseling practice

It is not easy to coin an easy definition of counseling. Many would say many things according to personal perceptions and experiences. We can only try to take a broader look into the various aspects and get a larger picture of the things that constitute what we call counseling. A definition has to be a brief, crisp and authoritative exposition of the meaning and nature or scope of something in a minimum of words. The type of search we are exploring does not fit in with a classical idea of definition. At the end of this exercise, we would end up with a larger understanding of counseling yet without a crisp definition! We attempt a definition here from what people expect and want counseling to be. We address many questions and in probing the questions and not in answering these questions, we get a larger picture of what the term stands for and what the ministry implies.

Some say counseling is helping, if so:

Is it helping to define the problem one faces? It is simple logic that when we try to handle a problem the handling would be meaningful as we have a definition to hold on. It is the very thing we are doing in trying to get a handle on the thing called 'definition'. The first step in problem-solving is defining the problem. But that is not the whole story.

Is it helping to acknowledge there is a problem that needs handling? Unless we acknowledge we have a problem there will be no motivation in making a beginning to handle the problem. Coming to the point of saying 'I have a problem' is the sign of growth. Bringing a person to that point is not easy. A Counselor can significantly contribute toward this growth in people.

Is it helping to own up responsibility to handle the situation?

If the growth ceases with acknowledging the problem, further growth would be stunted. For effective handling of a problem, the person has to arrive at a state of mind and be able to say, 'It is my responsibility to handle this'.

Is it helping to gather strength to deal with the problem?

Having said so much we would achieve nothing if we find ourselves sapped of all strength and not up to the task. This could be a disheartening moment. We need strength to handle our problems. Lack of strength and helplessness to really do something about our problems is very much the problem we started with. Helping to realize this indeed is a move toward growth.

Is it helping to find enough strength not to run away from problems?

When in such disheartening situations our normal tendency would be to run away from the problem. It is so much easier to do that. Counseling is for overcoming this moment when failure is staring down at us. A slight lift to resist the temptation from running away is also a counseling function.

Is it helping to come out with all the held up pains and fears?

Fear is the chief culprit here. Fear comes up with excuses to escape the struggles. Getting away from the problem definitely is an easier and comfortable option. So there is nothing surprising if we tend to adopt it. The awareness that this is a widespread phenomenon would assist the better handling of life issues.

Is it helping to identify the craving for procrastination?

We are upset about and fearful about what is going to happen. "Whatever it is, let me not precipitate it". If it can be kept at bay for some more time, let that be so. I do not want anyone to say "I messed it up". Let it simmer for the time'. That is our usual tactic, and that is nothing surprising.

Is it helping to get above the problems through resolving it?

Getting above the problem involves growing larger than the problem. That may not always be possible. But the love of our God is always larger than our problem. Getting above our problem is the natural route to the top, being in Him who is above the mundane.

Is it helping to identify the flaws in relating and relationships?

Many of our problems arise out of wrong relating and wrong relationships. What are the right premises to relate and build up relationships? When we look at relationships as means to personal gain and manipulate people involved to that end, a whole lot of unpleasant things happen. Counselors need to keep this in focus.

Is it helping to identify the urge to find fault with others?

There is so much relief to say and believe that all my problems are created by others. Professional comfort producers make people believe that their problems are in fact generated by other people, parents being the primary culprits. Those who hear this line love to hear that again and again. To be free from the responsibility for their situations is a largely releasing experience.

Is it helping to decipher the drive for pretension and deception?

Expanding the earlier point, we see most people enjoy the luxury of freedom from responsibilities. Men and women search high and low for scapegoats and for that they would adopt any measure including pretensions and deceptions of all descriptions. The counselor needs to keep that in mind.

Is it helping to find out reasons for relishing pride and conceit?

The inability to acknowledge responsibility very often is pride and pride bordering conceit. Many people have problems admitting they have problems. 'I am above all these. I am not like those others', is a typical Pharisaic attitude which can be described as 'holier-than-thou' nose-in-the-air postures. Let us be watchful for the signs of the upturned noses.

Is it helping to see clearly the pressing hurry to withdraw?

Taking a step back is an easier option in life. 'ICSC is too tough, you move out to State Syllabus' is a very usual piece of advice that poorer performers in Std. 8 and 9 get from some parents and teachers. That sort of attitude solidifies in other areas of life too. Withdrawal from a situation is less demanding. So much the better!

Is it helping to discover the eagerness to be critical?

This is another aspect of the tendency to find fault with others. Criticize others and make others feel less than us. Gosh! That is a great feeling. Add a touch of bitterness to it to feel more justified. Criticism is a contagion. It pollutes the very environment around the critic. It, in the end, poisons the critic in turn. Counselors need to recognize that and the poison-emitting critic.

Is it helping to understand the rush to be violent?

This is the opposite of being withdrawn. Those of the frustrated among us may not withdraw from confrontations. We as a race believe in doing things according to our own schemes to accomplish what we desire. We may say the philosophy of 'Karma' has no insignificant bearing on our thinking. The execution of an involved act generally ends up in violence. This also should be within the field of vision of the counselor.

Is it helping to get a better understanding of one's own situation?

Lack of strength to handle the problems in life, fear, tendency to procrastinate, faulty relationships, finding fault, pretensions, pride, the critical vein in us, tendency to withdraw or be violent and many other of our inclinations may remain covered up. We may knowingly or unknowingly refuse to accept our roles in relation to our situations.

Is it helping to let go of fear?

As we have seen, fear is a pervasive emotion, quite powerful, as we know. It can immobilize and rob mature thinking. Fear is a master and is adept at taking away reasoning capacity. Where there is fear, hesitation rules and indecision is the order of the day. There is one place where there is no fear. That place is the bosom of the Father whom he knows as 'perfect love'. The counselor has to minister in love to help to let go of fear.

Is it helping to handle fear, anger, guilt, shame, anxiety, addiction and the rest of it?

Helping to handle fear alone may fall short of a sense of holistic wellbeing. Anger, guilt, anxiety, addictions are serious stumbling-blocks in the progressive growth and wellbeing of human beings. A single negative emotion can pollute the entire life scene. Presence of the Holy, Whole, Perfect God in the life of a person is the means to freedom from all negatives. Let the person dwelling in negatives know that truth.

Is it helping to take a fresh look and see the unseen? Jesus said, 'Let those who have eyes see'. This is not an easy thing, yet so vital in experiencing and interpreting life. Even with functional eyes, we do not really see. We engage in the act of looking and fail to 'see'. We look and take in what we like to see, not always what we ought to see. Jesus said, 'Lo, I am with you always, till the end of age'. If we do not see Him it is not because He is a liar, but a serious personal spiritual myopia.

Is it helping to get a total sense of all things without distortions?

There is no disputing that man is an intelligent being, and he is superbly capable of twisting and entwining events and instances for the sake of individual comfort. Man then comes up with new creative ideas which would be of personal convenience and comfort producing. If these contortions violate normal moral lines and social norms, sorry, that is the problem of the observer. Man is capable of infinite distortions and manipulations. The counselor needs to be a straight-shooter with considerable knack to disclose the truth in love.

If so, is it helping toward healing and wholeness?

The end goal in all counseling is wholeness in tune with The Whole. A counselor is expected to be wise enough to recognize what is less than whole and should be in touch with the whole to lead the degenerated to wholeness. There is nothing even suggestive of an easy handling of distorted lives to wholeness in the ministry of love. The counselor needs to keep that very much in mind. He has an almost impossible task, yet all things are possible in Him who the counselor serves.

Some others say it is teaching; if so;

Is it teaching the inevitability of problems/conflicts in all life situations?

Conflict is implicit in all human situations. The ideal and perfect place without any trace of problems is gone for good from early in the history of mankind. There is no return to that while on earth. Man should grow large enough to accept this truth. It is the counselor's responsibility to reveal this bit of eternal truth to people in conflicts. The peace about the truth of the moment can calm down the troubled heart. May the counselor herself/himself be wiser to this sobering fact!

Is it teaching to discover the dynamics of self-inflicted suffering?

We actively contribute a further humbling truth that we fabricate and perpetuate most problems in our personal, family, communal, social situations. It is also a fact that we generally lack the integrity to own up our own contributions. A gentle, accepting, understanding counselor would be able to tactfully put it across. The act of putting it across is of pivotal importance. That is one of the places where 'who the counselor is' assumes crucial significance.

Is it teaching that the preliminary steps are resolving what to do and then doing it?

It is not always realistic to expect that every counselee be well-informed about the practical and feasible initial steps to resolve life situations. Educative counseling is an integral part of this ministry. The counselor should be adept in the judicious exercise of this aspect of counseling. It goes without saying a counselor should not venture out into counseling without proper training in the discipline.

Is it teaching to discern the purpose behind suffering?

There are no wasted events in the divine economy. 'All things work together for the good of those who love God' is an irrefutable and repeatedly proven reality in the lives of those who love the Lord. Yet it is hard even for those believers to accept it as the suffering is ongoing. It calls for a greater degree of faith and interpretative skills to discern the real purpose behind suffering. Not easy, yes the counselor can help with her/his store of God's provisions in adversity.

Is it teaching that hasty and illogical acts only compound an already complex problem?

Confusion is the reigning monster at times of intense and often contrived happenings. Straight thinking becomes a casualty leading to hurried illogical acts with inevitable and sad outcomes. A counselor needs to exercise moderation and be unhurried throughout the execution of wise steps discerned in the divine guidance prompted by the Holy Spirit. Take extra care not to disregard the Divine in preference to personal positions.

Is it teaching to always look for alternatives when faced with tough situations?

The counselor needs to learn from lowly organisms. Observe the ants and know how they tackle obstructions in their way. Pushing against a blank wall is not the wisest thing to do. Yet very many of us evidence mulish obstinacy. That is hardly the way to handle real life situations.

Is it teaching to use one's intellect and see scientifically all aspects of a problem situation?

Observation, inference, planning, synergizing, execution, adaptation, valuation are sensible steps in handling tough situations. I believe teaching to really 'see' is a big issue in counseling. Many do not 'see' despite looking. Many more refuse to see, in spite of looking. Some are stone blind. The discerning counselor has a tough job and should have the assurance that it would be accomplished in the grace of God.

Is it teaching the inevitability of pain when moving against nature's laws?

By now the counselor knows what she/he has opted to do is no mean thing. She/he knows what pain is and its various harsh shades. Ordinarily men and women want to hold on to their angularities and keep to their self-assured routes even when it becomes obvious they are defeating themselves. Ushering in bits of humility to come to a point of gratitude for all that is about is by no means a cheap act. Yet that is what a counselor has to do!

Is it teaching that one comes to reap a whirlwind in time, if one sows wind?

Common sense loses its grip when quick and easy gains entice people from the other bank where the grass is always greener. Many lives go down the drain crossing over to the quick and becoming dead in the going. The counselor has a better and wiser hold on God and life, and she/he can do a world of difference to the 'sower' of wind that they may be spared of the plight to reap whirlwinds.

Is it teaching that thistle and fig cannot grow from the same bough?

There definitely is no doubt that a vast part of counseling (especially in youth, pre- marital and family counseling) is predominantly informing, educating as the occasion calls for. Even good and godly people resort to evil when captivated by an ideology or fixation on personal gains. The Roman soldiers and the Jewish crowd who crucified Christ Jesus consisted of loving fathers, husbands, and sons. A counselor's function includes providing a reflecting surface for the counselees to get a true picture of themselves in the foreground of their background situations. Remember the background makes the foreground clearer but it does not determine the content.

Is it teaching how to handle fear, anger, anxiety, guilt and the rest of it?

A fearful animal is charged to do the illogical. Anger is a manifestation of most negative thoughts. Guilt/shame/remorse proceeds from acts committed in anger. Unforgiveness and/or violence would be a further complication. A wise counselor should know this and have the facility to lead the erring individual to safer premises.

Is it teaching the outcomes in unfounded suspicions?

Faced with no clear answers for troubling questions in life and when an individual inevitably fails to get a satisfactory answer for the 'whys' in life, suspicion is the easiest resort to hide in. There the individual hatches out sinister plots to raise scapegoats for taking the blame for 'my situation'. These sorts of wild escapades produce wounds left, right and center. The counselor's role is unenviable, yet you are required to bring in sense where reason is on furlough.

Is it teaching the art of looking beyond oneself and seeing the real world of suffering?

Myopia is far more widespread than we would like to think. Many of us do not see beyond our nose. Even the nose will not be seen if we try to look at the nose alone. 'My pain' is naturally more painful. Compassion is easy to be contained only in thoughts yet it can be indicated objectively. That is famously possible in the life of the Man of sorrows, Jesus the Christ, which should be familiar to the counselor.

Is it teaching that laziness is a willful choice?

Scott Peck succinctly expressed laziness as nothing short of sin in the book 'The road less traveled'. I believe no sin is involuntary though we would love to give it that hue. When an addict says, 'I am unable to stop my addiction', hear it as, 'I am not bothered enough to stop now'. People might say you have a hearing problem. Let that be so! All the same, it is a choice to continue in sin which is ably assisted by laziness. You would be wiser to keep that in mind.

Is it teaching that knowledge is acquired, but pure wisdom comes from above?

Pure knowledge by itself in man would produce more of a Frankenstein. Wisdom belongs to a different species. Knowledge and emotions in their joint endeavor produce confusion, whereas wisdom emerges from the interaction of knowledge with the faith system. It is somewhat complicated to explain here in the context of this question. Suffice to remember pure wisdom comes from above (James.1).

Is it teaching the virtue of forgiveness?

An unforgiving heart is a furnace. It consumes from within causing shriveling and ultimate crumbling from which there is no escape in time. The counselor should know this more as a person who has enjoyed the sweet taste of forgiveness received and given. A poor technician may know the theory on forgiveness but a person who has an estimation of the priceless blood of the Lamb that was bled for him would be the right person to share the beauty of forgiveness.

Is it teaching forgiveness paves the way for enriched relationships?

'No man is an island' is a well-known axiom. Bridges have to be built between individuals for a community to happen with persons, not just individuals. I say this because, in my understanding, an individual incapable of forming relationships fails to become a person. Again space constraints limit me here. But let me try to give one example. The woman at the well was living as an individual though doing her own thing. She turns into a person in her encounter with Jesus.

Is it teaching that there is healing in forgiveness?

We keep coming back to forgiveness, as it is the harbinger of resurrected power in man. An unforgiving person is a sick entity, burning inside, crumbling outside, and perishing in a hurry. There is only one way out of it. Exercise forgiveness knowingly blessing to be blessed and healed in turn. There are no shortcuts. That is a lesson made poignantly explicit from the cross.

Is it teaching that there is always hope even in the most hopeless situations?

I would like to respond to that question with a one-word answer 'YES'. The Counselor should always speak the language of hope. Her/his very vocabulary should be such that hope should be reflected in every world for she/he serves a God who is equal to any impossible situation. An extended arm parted the Red Sea. The counselor need not be hesitant to ask most largely believing there is no impossible situation. Apparent hopelessness is a passing phenomenon.

Is it teaching that healing and wholeness come from the Healer and the "ONE' who is whole?

The answer again obviously is a simple 'YES'. The troubled person is in need of healing. That person in 'dis' 'ease' is running around healing contrivances, potions and people. She/he keeps asking 'where will deliverance come from?' Pointing the searcher in the direction and leading her/him to the source of healing is one of the prime functions of a counselor. Do please learn that and do that for sure.

Is it teaching the truth 'apart from Me you can do nothing?'[95] (John.15:5)

The truth 'apart from Christ Jesus nothing gets done' should be understood by the counselor as 'apart from Christ Jesus (incarnate Love) no counseling does happen'. As far as Christian counseling is concerned that is the absolute truth for the counselor. Believing that in personal conviction is one thing, but teaching that to a troubled person is a different cup of tea. Only a counselor who lives and practices 'abiding' would be able to pass it on as an uplifting experience.

Is it teaching that the hope of man's glory is; God; the Love-Truth in man?

Man by himself and in himself is a limited entity.[96] Psalm 8:4 is a revealing text. We love to pretend we are in control. We act as if we are. Most often, we act like the ground warbler which thinks it is shaking the earth when it rocks its tail end. A Christian counselor's worth is who he is by virtue of who he is in.[97] Colossians 1:27 makes that amply clear.

Is it also teaching to perceive the unseen?

In counseling as in everyday life, things move on without coming into our field of vision. There are many more things directly behind our field of vision. A counselor needs to have a sense of the unseen. For people with 20/20 vision this idea is hard to grasp. When we close our eyes and move about, we begin to get a sense I refer to. The other side of this happening is that we can develop an uncanny sense of the unseen. The counselor needs to have the facility to 'perceive the unseen'.

Is it further teaching that 'By His power that is at work within you, He can make you do far more exceedingly beyond anything you ask or even think?'

This has an obvious reference to[98] Ephesians 3:20 and that forms the backbone of what we do in counseling in His name. His power operates in us enabling us to do 'far more exceedingly than anything we ask or even imagine'. The counselor needs that sort of strength, for the life situations of people who come for counseling can at times only be described as 'impossible'. If that is so, by teaching alone, would healing and wholeness visit the troubled? It is yet one more question which begets an answer in the negative. Much more than helping and teaching it is necessary to usher in wholeness. Then there are those who say counseling is encouraging, if so,

Is it encouraging taking a look at one's own naked self?

Not many people have the guts and the facility to take an honest look at oneself. They are skeptical of what they might come across in themselves. Or it may be pure ignorance or lack of enlightenment. Unless I see myself in a mirror I have no idea of my ugliness or otherwise. Normal human tendency is to believe that I am the best specimen around in a long time. Do be a 'mirror' to gently reveal a real reflection of the naked self of the person you are dealing with.

Is it encouraging coming down from the lofty moral perches of one's own design?

Playing the 'holier-than-thou' game is quite exciting and self-validating. Getting up on to a podium and preaching down to the trapped; messages of liberation is more exciting and self-satisfying. It improves the self-image. After the preaching, a long- winded sermon on the need for moral concerns and commitment, the preacher can feel superior. This could become a trap in the counselor's life as much as it could be a problem for some counselees.

Is it encouraging dumping all inferior feelings as an 'accepted in the beloved'?

Many people come for counseling with pronounced feelings of rejection: 'No one loves me. I am not good enough to be loved by anyone. I have no lovable qualities. I do not deserve to be loved'. People who feel they are not loved and cherished think in this manner. The truth is far from it. Jesus loves and accepts all. There is no partiality in His love. The troubled person has no accessible means to know this on a personal level. The counselor is in an eminent position to introduce this love to the person in the throes of rejection, not with meaningless rhetoric but with the loving ways and concern with which the counselor deals with the counselee.

Is it also encouraging knowing the Truth, that the Truth shall set the bound free?

Falsehood binds. Untruths are bondages. Wherever human transactions are carried out the danger of wielding untruths is a distinct possibility. When a human being operates from a private agenda of personal profit, the temptation to flaunt untruth is implicit. Morality and truthfulness get to have the back burners where profit is a fixation. Know this and take care to set the bound free from the bondages of untruths. Bondages will keep the bound in darkness. Freedom is an experienced blessing in truth.

Is it encouraging to evidence justice and humility in relationships?

Relationships are soured when proud and haughty interactions take the upper hand. The very basis of Christian relationships is the sense of shared oneness in Christ. We all are branches of the same True Vine. How sad it is when some of us resort to pretensions and try to establish we are somehow 'more equal' than others. If a Christian counselor reduces herself/himself to this pattern of thinking; that counselor would do more damage to the counselee than good. Humility and justice in the counselor's interactions should be demonstrably seen by the counselee.

Is it encouraging dropping all pretensions and calculations in relationships?

We have seen elsewhere in this book that there can be no love in calculations. It is worth repeating that 'a calculating person can never be open to love'. Calculations look for gains in some form or the other. A counselor reduced to calculating would tend to run her/his business for profit even in a counselor-counselee relationship, all the time giving an impression she/he has the good of the counselee in focus. This deception would not go far with the cheated. The counselor's responsibility is to encourage the counselee to understand pretensions and calculations are curare-tipped arrows.

Is it also encouraging the counselee to forgive without keeping count?

There is resurrection power in forgiveness. We keep coming back to forgiveness only because of its huge bearing on total healing. Forgiveness enables us to bury the past. Nothing of the past is taken into active ongoing scores to be settled. A forgiving person would resemble the Lord Jesus on the cross. It is from there He offered disarming, almost impossible forgiveness to all His accusers and persecutors. What a great lesson from the cross. For all those who consider the cross as the symbol of salvation, forgiveness is the quickening content of the cross leading to resurrection.

Is it encouraging at a shared meal or walking the extra mile?

I have the incident of the Lord walking along with the two disciples on the road to Emmaus, as I present this idea to you. As a counselor, you need to find time and enjoy spending it with those whom you care for. The beauty of Christian counseling is that as a Christian counselor you are a caring person, and you would be disposed to take on the extra burden to encourage your counselees to see the truth. The idea is you need to be such a person, open, to be of encouragement.

Is it encouraging to trust in the omnipotent, omniactive, omnipresent, and omniscient God?

A person in trouble at times tends to doubt and distrust. Some discouraging remarks or acts from others cause the distressed person to look at others with suspicion. There is an apprehension that generally people are not trustworthy. 'After all, why should they? They find nothing of gain in me'. The counselor in her/his dealing with the counselee brings it out. It is futile to trust in man, but we can trust God our maker and redeemer in all circumstances, in all places and at all times.

Is it encouraging becoming like a child to inherit heaven on earth?

A Christian counselor's obligation toward a counselee is measured in terms of the inheritance the counselor has received from God. A counselor can share only from the fullness of the heavenly provisions. He has nothing of his own. Yet he can lead the counselee to the source and help him turn an inheritor of heavenly provisions. Not many counselors may see his obligation to the counselee in this dimension. But the Christian position is exactly that. You as a Christian counselor need to keep this aspect in focus and lead the counselees to the inheritance.

Is it encouraging looking and really seeing the One who stands at the door and knocks?

Jesus stands at the door of every heart gently knocking as described in [99]Revelation 3:20. He says, 'Behold.....'. That is the problem with many of us. We need to look and see the One who is waiting at the doorstep of our hearts. Pressed from all sides with burdens of everyday life which is at best a rat-race, no one has the time and inclination to 'waste time' looking for something not easily seen. The Christian counselor has the almost impossible task to calm down the people in a hurry and prompt them to take a believing look which would generate a 'My Lord and my God' response. Some degree of self-revelation of your experiencing this is called for at this point.

Is it encouraging hearing the inaudible knock?

This point is also somewhat the same as the one above. Looking for something not easily seen is essentially the same as listening to something which is not easily heard. The seeing and hearing I refer to here happen in an inner ambience of faith which does not happen before a trusting relationship is built-up between the counselor and counselee.

A cardinal principle we have emphasized earlier has a strong bearing here. Counseling is not so much what the counselor does but who the counselor is.

Is it encouraging taking the right path and right direction to the right goal in life at the right time?

People who have lost direction and ambled into the confusing jungle of misdeeds at the end of their tether come seeking the counselor. In the hands of a counselor who is smart about the world with the right jargon and facility with high sounding techniques, the counselee can be twirled to fit into the counselor's designs. This might sound a bit too far fetched. Truth is stranger, brother. Your commitment is to lead your counselee in a direction that is right for the person and in agreement with the indwelling Holy Spirit, leaving your own self-induced ideas aside calls for humility of a higher order.

Is it encouraging reaching out and touching the hem of His garment?

You as a Christian counselor are convinced of the source of healing. You are a healed person. That is my assumption. If not, be healed before dealing with the people who approach you for counseling. Be on your knees and in prayer; reach out to the hem of His garment. 'Lo I am with you always, till the end of ages' is not an empty promise. None of His promises is empty. As the one who had touched Him, you are in the eminent position to encourage others to do that.

Is it encouraging and convincing that 'a broken and contrite heart, He will not forsake?'

The fifty-first Psalm came from the heart of a person who knew and believed the content of what he said. He vividly experienced it and in course became a man closer to the heart of God, I believe, mainly based on his unabashed repentance and readiness to be cleansed. Unacknowledged sin may well be the cause for the confusion, failure and suffering. This possibility cannot be ruled out as a matter of insignificance. The counselor needs to be wiser and be able to present the validity of the broken and contrite heart in counseling.

Is it encouraging hearing the words 'Come unto me all who are weary and heavily laden?'

[100]Matthew 11:28 is a verse so widely and routinely used in Christian circles that has lost its edge? People have problems responding to an invitation of this sort unless they are familiar with the inviting person. Your counselee may not have even heard of Jesus, the person extending this incredible invitation. As a Christian counselor, you have the enviable privilege to introduce this marvelous person you know personally. Again, the great principle comes into play. Who you are would be the deciding factor with the person who you counsel in going to the One you introduce.

Is it also encouraging hearing the rest of it, "I will give you rest"?

It is the second part of the invitation. It goes without saying that unless one goes to Jesus in response to the invitation it would be impractical to receive the rest on promise. When the first part is heeded to then the second part is easier to comply with. If the counselor is seen as a person who enjoys peace despite prevailing circumstances, the counselee would only be happy to be at the receiving end. Again, it depends on your humble reflection of His presence and the person you are.

If so, will encouragement be an end in itself ensuring healing and wholeness?

Counseling is not a single window corporate business transaction. That is why we are finding it so hard to arrive at a one-sentence definition. Some rightly say counseling is comforting.

Is it comforting by offering a shoulder to cry on?

A shoulder to cry on definitely is a comfort. Whether a counselor is required to offer that is something determined by the way the counselor finds comfort in his moments of anguished pain. A Christian is familiar with the pierced hand that is extended to embrace and comfort. A person thus comforted is an effective agent to lead others to experience the same comfort. However, for a Christian it is a mandate that he comforts all others who are in all sorts of discomfort with the same comfort with which he himself is comforted. This is a principle we have stated at several places because this is the cornerstone of Christian meta-love-counseling.

Is it comforting by wiping tears away?

While wiping tears is comforting as we all know and do, the Lord has exemplified another aspect of crying. He did not do away with the need to cry. Crying has healing, lifting, and releasing properties too. Crying is evidence of hurt, loss and repentance. Everything including repentance does not go unnoticed and un-responded. There is always room for a hearty meaningful tear that would be wiped away by the all-seeing God. Comforting a person in pain has to be done in an appropriate manner knowing what causes the pain. Hurt. loss, fear, guilt, self-pity, cheating, betrayal, the unexpected, remorse, real repentance all may generate tears. Sense deeply and respond appropriately either facilitating or wiping as necessary.

Is it crying with those who cry and laughing with those who laugh?

Responding appropriately is a finely tuned affair. Gross reactions would be misunderstood and taken offense at. Your sensitivity is vital in striking a resonating cord with your counselee. Remember you are not a professional with a standardized and fixed interactive procedural drill. I am thinking of the fixed labored smile of an air hostess or a front-office receptionist with professional compulsions. Anyone can see through that sort of smile. Do be Christ-like and reflect Him in all your dealings, especially in counseling with people.

Is it praying for and praying with those who suffer?

One enduring and functional tool for effective Christian counseling is prayer. The life of the Christian is linked to that of his Lord with prayer. It is through prayer that all things beyond our asking and imagining happen by His power that works in us. In prayer, we have access to the greatest treasures of mercy and grace of the Lord. There is nothing magical that happens in Christian counseling other than answered prayers. Everything miraculous that transpires in counseling is in and through prayer. The power of prayer needs to be seen and valued with all the reverence it deserves.

Is it comforting in the assurance that help is nearby and available?

The Christian has help available at short notice for the Christian; help is only a prayer away. Your counselee may not contribute to your ideas about prayer. But that really does not matter. Prayers are not answered on our terms. The Lord hears and He responds in His time and according to His purposes which would always be for our good, though it may not appear so for the expectant observer. But the believing Christian knows that all things work together for the good for those who love the Lord. The counselor needs to cash in on that promise and make it available to the counselee.

Is it comforting simply by offering to be with those in pain in times of grief?

There is nothing more reassuring than being with, in times of grief and pain. No one generally likes to take any long time for being with and being in a comforting mood unless the person is a close relative or an intimate friend. It is demanding and draining to be comforting others in painful circumstances. But counseling is a willful interpathic choice wherein one has to be generous with time and be a source of comfort to others. Just being with others and assuring them that you are with them in their pain-filled circumstances through your words and acts is a great relief for those in pain.

Is it offering to share the comfort you yourself enjoy in the Real Comforter?

This is in direct reference to[101] 2 Corinthians 1:3, 4 which we have referred to in many other places also. In a way, these verses form the bedrock of the discipline of Christian counseling. The counselor has nothing of his own to give by way of comfort unless there is an overflow of comfort in his life that he receives from the Father of all comfort[102]. 'My cup runneth over' Ps.23:5 (KJV) is absolutely dependable

Is it comforting through touching the untouchable?

Many people, more than we usually consider likely, strain under the pressure of rejection and abandonment. They rightly or wrongly think they are not loved, not needed, not cherished, not cared for, and not valued. Experiences of rejection are hugely painful syndrome, and in trying to find release from such pains people go on committing utterly foolish things to gain acceptance. They need acceptance, and they crave to be loved. The sad fact is there are so few who would bother to look at them, care for and validate them. As a counselor, your moral duty is to validate people, and the easiest thing to do is to love others as Jesus loves you. He did not hesitate to touch me! So what should be my response to that!

Is it comforting through sharing the burdens of the burdened?

[103] Galatians 6:2 lays it down: 'Bear the burdens of others and thus fulfill the law of Christ'. Counseling is a means to fulfill the law of Christ. A Christian counselor has no way out of

that honorable responsibility. Bearing a burden is making the burden lighter through sharing the weight of the burden and affording a breathing space for the struggling person to get a firm foothold. That is interpathy in action. Through this the counselee is allowed time to grow and grow large enough to be equal to the pressures of life. The assurance that the counselor is a reflective presence at hand to be of support in times of need is in itself a great comfort facilitating growth under the circumstances.

Is it comforting by assurance of forgiveness even for grievous sins?

People struggle under guilt and burdens of what they call mistakes and wrong doings. At the most, they might say, they have done some foolish things. However, they have no concept of sin, or they might deliberately interpret their doings as legitimate and call it by euphemistic names offering sin desired justifications. The erring folks have a problem calling a spade, a spade. But their release would be enormous when they realize there is forgiveness in Jesus for every sin even of any red variety. Lead them to receive forgiveness in Christ.

Is it comforting to hold on to see the emerging victory in change through repentance?

Repentance is a harbinger of cleansing, and this cleansing happens because of the faithfulness of the One who forgives. The Christian is familiar with the disarming forgiveness of the One who forgives and introduces this Great Forgiver to those under the burdens of sin. The Christian counselor stands a victor through the forgiveness received and is in an ideal position to offer comfort based on that solid experience of forgiveness received.

Is it offering comfort in the revelation that one's own suffering is puny compared to others?

We know a centripetally growing individual focuses on the self, lives for self, and is in a serious effort to contain self efforts within, giving out nothing of the self. This individual sees only his problems, relates only with his pains, glues himself onto his suffering and in the process makes a mountain out of his private molehills. His experience of suffering is so huge, his pains so insufferable that his eyes are blind to realities outside him. He is the proverbial frog in the well. The counselor has to help to 'open' this individual's eyes to see the realities and widespread suffering around.

Is the comforting assurance in an organic oneness with Jesus a granted fact?

That is the essence of Christian Meta-love-counseling. The utmost in the experience of comforting is the proximity to the source of comfort. The counselee has lost comfort and has come to you to gain it. As a comforted counselor, you are in contact with the source of all comfort and are placed in an eminent position to lead the counselee to an abiding relationship with Jesus; the source. Christian meta-love-counseling is never a bipartite A–B linear interaction where neither one is in control of the interaction. Christian meta counseling counseling is very much a tripartite communion wherein the base angles A–B are connected and blessed by the 'C' at the vertex factor from the top forming a stable union.

Is it finding comfort in the fact that anything asked for in the name of the Son will be received?

People work through to get at and work for receiving comfort. We strive to carve out a comfortable niche that would be the coziest corner on earth. This is very human. Asking the Son for anything has a condition attached to it; ask it right and ask for the purposes of God for us. That is legitimate asking which would be supplied in His time beyond our very imagination. We need to have the forethoughts to know His will and the humility to accept His will. Abiding comfort is not a quick-fix given for the casual and greedy asking. The only condition is: 'Abide and be able to do all things'.

Is it finding comfort in the fact that we live because HE lives?

Hurting people have a pressing common need. They keep looking out to receive that comfort from anywhere or anyone ready to offer it. Real comfort comes only from trusting in God who only can offer lasting comfort, what I would call the Abiding comfort. Pain and tragic events are not signs of indifference from God. Like the father of the Prodigal son, God the Father is grieving with us. He loves us and would never forsake or leave us. Right in the midst of a hurting community, the Christian counselor has the function to become a comforter representing and reflecting Christ. The Christian meta-love-counselor's heart has to be tender and compassionate in the effervescing comfort of His Lord and Master Jesus Christ.

Is acquired comfort meant to be the final solution to experience healing and wholeness?

We are ready to pay through our noses for a branded product, even if it is an imitation. People are happy with imitation Rolexes from Super Shoppe sold for less than Rs.5, 000/-; a Pierre Cardin imitation belt for Rs.100/-. We like to have our labels outside which are in ghastly taste, though the normal practice now. Acquired comfort is cheap, yet worthless in an abiding sense. The Christian can lead a thirsting counselee to the river of living waters to be filled and comforted abidingly. Christian meta-love-counseling therefore, is an act of the constraining love of Christ. This might appear as a one sentence definition. The problem is 'LOVE'; it is a many faceted thing, the epistemology of which is way beyond human comprehension and not amenable to a simple definition. If we can define LOVE in one sentence, we have a private, convenient and complying god in our pocket. People love to have such gods, and we have an excess of those springing up left, right and center!

This is the kind of love we are talking about – not that we once upon a time loved God, but that he loved us and sent His Son as a sacrifice to clear away our sins and the damage they have done to our relationship with[104] God (I John 4, The Message).

PETAL-18

META-LOVE-COUNSELING IS

The very term meta-love-counseling, implies a form of counseling beyond the ordinary concept of counseling in its traditional garb. Any counseling done within a framework of LOVE-TRUTH (Love-Truth is the term I employ to understand God as such) will have positive outcomes. Meta-love-counseling goes into the finer nuances of the LOVE-TRUTH that is functionally operative in it; impossible as it may seem. It reiterates the dictum that what is impossible for man is possible for God when God uses man for His purposes. There is no reason to doubt that His power would be denied to the believing servant in furthering His purposeful intentions.

It is an unbelievably hard fact to accept the proposition that the Meta-clove-counselor can sense all phenomena around, that is; see, touch, hear, smell and taste in a holistic sense beyond the ordinary. As in the case of Agape love referred to earlier, this wholeness we refer to as a presence in the human level, has imperfections and can only be understood and internalized in its manifestation. This presence is singularly and selflessly loving, thinking fairly, creatively intelligent, fearlessly beneficial, largely accepting, bravely building up, indiscriminately tolerant, keenly compassionate and humbly witnessing. Again this presence is unassumingly serene, with no anxiety or guilt. Such wholeness can only be a significantly exclusive spiritual attribute. A high degree of personal holiness in purity is needed. This descriptive elaboration need not to be frighteningly unrealistic, because it is not a labored acquisition. I have said and keep saying met-love-counseling is nothing other than a spiritual endowment to a loving, sensitive counselor. It is not super consciousness as some mind technicians maintain. It is not a technique. It is an endowment which need not generate any skepticism about its possibility within the reach of any God fearing believing individual.

The whole essence of it is; it is a given.

God can work only through His people and you definitely are one of them if you are taking time to devote to this approach. Believe and see the wonder of it all happening through you and any firm believer in the divine context.

Here we may come across some roadblocks, that are our flawed understanding of what and who is God. For the primitive man god is a frightening, intimidating, even monstrous god like the calamitous nature and the wild forces. That god requires pacification and worshipful submission to avoid mishaps and to beneficially guide the destinies. The methods of revering such ideation may differ from culture to culture and regions to regions and from primitive to evolved religion to religions.

But man has also started of old knowing and interacting with a God who is Love. This God needs to be conceptualized and internalized as a Love-Truth in life, which is formless and beyond imagination. Something or someone that can be imagined needs to take a form; has to have a form for man to get a hold on as god. We need to know and interact with God who is Love-Truth and only in love there can be understanding which is considered meta-love-cognition enabling meaningful knowing of Love itself.

He, who knows Love-Truth, knows how to lovingly respond to life. Those who exist in the subjective, searching and analytical mode of existence are more often incapable of responding in love as they have a personal agenda for gain in one form or another. They are likely to react in evident manners or suppress the reaction within causing further suffering. Reactions are not preceded by thoughts but kicked up by instinctive drives for instant gratification. Reactions are always in anger; but responses invariably are always in love. Consequences in the two types of interactions are only imaginable.

Anger is not a comfortable answer for any situation in life whereas a loving response is the sign of maturity and godliness. Emotionally driven lives cannot be open for the revealing truth, vital in the imminent moment. The ability to respond in love is the mark of personal growth. Such capacity to knowingly turn away from anger goes side by side with such maturing growth. There is underlying godliness and metacognition of the presence of Love-Truth, that is; God within. A major part of the beginning of the healing process in Meta-love-counseling depends on raising to the state of being in which God is an all round palpable Love-Truth for the person in need for healing.

A Meta-love-counselor needs to see that which really 'IS'; the truth in any given situation. Let me try to illustrate. One evening as I was going out for a walk, I saw a young man known to me, in obvious inebriation, zigzagging the road and coming toward the direction I was heading. He was at risk of being run over in the heavy traffic. Realizing the danger I stopped where I was and waited for him to come nearer. Then I approached him and gently told him of the possible danger in the heavy traffic and offered him a lift to his home. He then floundered into a kind of tottering stop and looked into my face. He followed it up with slurred filthy abuses, questioning my ancestry and my business with him. He asked me "Does this road belong to your father?" and followed it up with slushy, stinking words. For a moment I lost bearing of the reality of the moment and caught hold of his collar with my left hand to give him a whack with my right hand. He held my left hand with his right hand and was groping at his waistband with his left hand, probably for a knife or something which he may have had with him.

Right at the moment a friend from the opposite side happened on the scene broadly smiling at the drama. I smiled too. Stroking his head with my right hand in a blessing manner I let the young person go with gentle concerned advice to be careful.

In a fit of reactive anger I lost touch with the truth of the moment and was about to act unwisely. The reality was plain as day. The young man was totally inebriated. Angry reaction could only vitiate the scene. Loving response called for leading the young man in acceptance of the reality and the need for leading him to safety in love. A generous loving smile took care of a possible nasty scene.

On the other hand, I felt insulted and reactive and failed to understand the truth. It was emotion that led me into a near disaster. It is understandable the young man was in no shape to know the reality and let alone the truth of the moment. Reaction took over and I missed the opportunity to be a blessing in the situation. I took his freedom to react as license for me to ignore the truth and react in turn. But that taught me a valuable lesson in being a blessing in whatever situation that I may happen to be in. Had I invited him and lovingly led him to my home, given time to rest and a glass of water or something, he would have cooled down and got home in a cooler and sober manner. It would have taken me some trouble to go to that extent and get him cooled enough to proceed home more safely. But my mode was reactive and counterproductive. I lost sight of the Love-Truth that should have been guiding me in love. My mere being with him and accepting his situation would have ushered in some healing touch beyond my imagination. Analysis of the incident helped me to get the inkling that God's grace will be missed if we become blind to the truth of the moment; the truth that I missed in this case.

A primary pre-requisite in receiving healing in meta-love-counseling is the ability of the counselee in the art of responding-in-Love which is an existential requirement for any one desiring a peaceful and calm life style. A Major concern of the Meta-love-counselor ought to be easing the counselee into the art of responding. Adopting a lifestyle of responding-in-love is not as hard as it may appear from a distance.

So, it goes without saying, if the recipient needs to be in a responding-in-love mode of existence how much more the Meta-love-counselor ought to be in the Love-Truth-blessing-state! That exactly is the crux of the whole process. Clambering into a reacting-in-anger mode of life is easier, quicker and instantaneous. Absorbing or administering harm is quicker in execution because thinking is not part of that emotion driven process. Reacting is bent on inflicting and countering assault.

But sharing and spreading of love may take a while as deeper physical, mental and spiritual processes are involved in it. Responding-in-love is more concerned with giving only, blessing in essence. It fears no rebuttals. The disposition to respond-in-love is a grace-gift from God

The moment we acknowledge the fact that God is Love-Truth; God turns formless, because we cannot assign a form to Love and Truth, both of which are qualities. For the ordinary individual the idea of a formless God is incomprehensible. Our imaginations play around forms and formal phenomena. A god conceived in my imagination and given form in my mind is more available for appeasing and appropriating as per my own specification which in course of time stands the chance to predicate a mental or physical form in others too. For instance, the idea of acquisition can take the form of a god in me and then, there could be others who might find it a profitable path to their kind of god too. An individual taking on a form of deity, putting on appropriate acts, pieces of clothing, chanting ritualistic chants to please the listener can very easily turn himself or herself into a god-individual, despicable as it is. These things happen. But such are not be on the healing scene

Love, Joy, Patience, Kindness, Goodness, Faithfulness, Gentleness, Self-control, Acceptance, Humility, Tolerance, Compassion and Truth and all such godly qualities are palpable in a realizable sense only. But to have a sense of the formless and be comfortable with its existential validity, man has to develop and elevate the consciousness to be in union with the Love-Truth which can be safely acknowledged as God. A God-acknowledged man has no problem realizing God in the Universe. To put it differently, man acknowledges that God is the Omnipresence (present everywhere), Omniactive (present in all actions), Omnimorphic (present in all forms), Omniscient (all knowing), Omni Benedictio (blessing all), of the Omnipotent (all powerful), Omni-Omni (all and in all) Love-Truth that is realizable, though not phenomenally experienced. This unimaginable Love-Truth needs to be understood and clearly realized for man to have a sense of 'who' and what man is. In the absence of this Omni-Omni God, man is NOT; in the existential context, despite whatever the atheist may say. Meta-love-counselor is not a negotiable entity. He has observable integrity, inner and visible congruence and a peaceful countenance. A Meta-love-counselor needs to be leading a life in perfect inner and outer harmony not led into incongruence by slight shift in external or internal ambience. That is what we would designate a holistic life in total integration with what really 'IS'; the Love-Truth. Such a person only can function as a 'blessing presence'; so much in need as an envoy of healing-blessing-being.

The purpose of Meta Counseling is not only to relieve a person of the injuries from past or present but lead him to attain wholeness now. In practice of Metta-love-counseling one would come to realize that the chief pre-tempered tools available for the counseling process are dominantly meditation and prayer apart from the interpathic relating with the seeker or counselee.

Meditation and Prayer need to be understood slightly differently from the prevalent concept of commercial meditation popularized by ordinary vendors of comfort in the meditation market. We need to understand and practice a mode of meditation that leads to heightening of unadulterated awareness of and being in the moment.

Awareness cannot be captured and practiced. Awareness happens. More often when most people ordinarily refer to awareness, it lingers in a morphed/physical mode of existence. True awareness goes beyond the mere physical; encompassing the whole of the person; which means, the Body, Mind (Emotions, Intelligence and Volition) and Spirit. I said awareness happens and that is right, but prior to that we have to dump all mental content to create space for emptiness. That might sound like an unfamiliar term. Do keep in mind that our consciousness needs to be ready for the awareness to happen. Please mark the term 'Dump the Mental Content', which are essentially our thoughts and concerns. Should I vainly try to rig up a list of all concerns that infill our being? Some mundane examples to mention; like anxieties, boredom, calculations, judgment, defeats, envy, fears, guilt, hatred, shame, insecurity, unforgiveness, and jealousy; ad infinitum.

More than anything else the meta-love-counselor should exist in the moment bereft of cluttering thoughts and confusions to be enabled to be a source of blessing and healing to the needy. Though it might appear frighteningly impractical; the way to go about it is a simple and divinely enabling process, happening and not stage managed. This happens to anyone with an ardent commitment to bless. These concise simple seven steps in a nutshell will help for greater clarity.

1. Be still and KNOW and become AWARE of the Omnipresence of God right around you and within you in the silence of your heart.[105] (Ps.46:10)
2. Be ready to dump all metal content; thoughts and emotions[106] (Mat. 11:28)
3. Be in Him and be available to receive His holiness and purity[107]. (1 John. 3:3; 2 Pet.1:5-7)
4. Be receptive of the Holy Spirit and be in step with Holiness[108]. (Heb. 2:11)
5. Be thankful in total sense of gratitude.[109] (Col. 3:16)
6. Be a presence in His presence.[110] (Ps. 41:12)
7. Be comforted and be open to share the comfort.[111] (2 Cor.1:3-4)

Elaborations of these points are given variously in different parts of this book. They are not impossibly hard for a person willing to be a servant in and for Him, totally in His grace. Please note that they are about your being; a purely existential dimension. The effectiveness of the meta counselor is totally; finally, exclusively dependent on 'who' the meta counselor is - in Him- and not as much on what the meta-love-counselor does.

PETAL-19

HOW DOES IT WORK

In the first part there are a couple of short counseling instances, from personal experiences, bringing out a quality or a principle that is desirable in a meta-love-counselor. Experiences cannot be accepted as authentic and repeatable scientific facts. But do know that there is no claim that Meta-love-counseling and healing are scientific tools. Medical practice with the array of doctors, medicines, tools and all paraphernalia can bring about only 15% more 'good than bad' in disease management. At times great blessings happen in spite of the counselor. The prerogative always belongs to Christ Jesus who through the mediation of the Holy Spirit brings to pass all things bright and beautiful. It is not presented as a drill to be executed by the practicing meta-love-counselor. In the latter half there are thoughts to inspire and to ignite the imagination to appreciate the tremendous possibilities in a ministry aiming at sharing the healing and wholeness the meta-love-counselor experiences in the Lord of all comfort.

One inconvenient detail to keep in mind for the meta-love-counselor is to be existent on earth as a beneficial presence.

The meta-love-counselor has to be certainly a beneficial presence and beyond that. The meta-love-counselor must be infused with holiness. Lord Jesus implies in his saying that those who want to be a beneficial presence disbursing healing ought to be holy as He is holy[112] 1.Pet 1:15-16.

This state of being is hard to arrive at but not impossible in the grace of God. Holiness is not concocted or made up.

It (HOLINESS) again is a given in God's grace

Be assured that holiness in the meta-love-counselor happens when the counselor is a recipient of forgiveness from the Love-Truth. The forgiveness from Love-Truth is free once anyone with a repentant soul reaches out in earnest to the Love-Truth for forgiveness. Once forgiven your life starts on a fresh mandate with nothing of the past bothering you. You have come into real experience of holiness and purity. In that state of existence you are an effective tool in the hands of the Love-Truth who will eventually start using you as a vehicle for reaching healing to the troubled soul. Never think you are a slimy sinner any more. Your trust in the Love-Truth must be unshakable.

God's forgiveness is total and you are to be clean as a conduit of healing and comfort. This is nothing short of a miracle as all things that are in meta-love-counseling. The only thing to be watchful is that no act that would negate grace should happen in the life of a healer representing the Healer par excellence. Never doubt your eligibility as a healing agent on behalf of the Love-Truth. In meta-love-counseling you are not in it all alone. The comforting healing presence of God is within you beyond your understanding. Bothering to understand the dynamics of the Divine intervention in the meta-love-counseling process is not going to enhance the effectiveness of the whole process. Yield and let things happen beyond your analytical cognition because the happenings are in a meta-cognitive frame of events. The meta-love-counselor evolves as a 'presence' in living active presence of the Love-Truth.

Three instances of counseling

The Squabbling Couple

Half past 11 in the night I had this telephone call from a gentleman who was introduced to me a couple of days back. He was incoherent with a compelling sense of urgency. He was not screaming but was very loud and grossly crude totally incongruent with the content of his words. He said, "I need your help. Pray or come here. I am in trouble. My wife.....she says she is going to kill herself. Can you come now? Yes, she is here. Can you hear? She is crying. Can you talk to her? I want calm".

I asked the man to give the telephone to his wife. He did. There was crying and sobbing. I asked her gently to stand up and close her eyes. After that it seemed like an hour and a half. I asked her whether she would want me to pray for them. Again after it seemed to be an hour of another five minutes she almost inaudibly said, "Yes". I took my time, perhaps one to two minutes to say the next sentence. "Sister, if we have to receive any positive outcome through our prayer you have to hold the hand of your husband. I am in touch with you through this phone and the Lord God is amidst us in this. Would you hold the hands of your husband now?" I thought I lost her. Time ticked on and possibly after another very long, perhaps three to four minutes the husband said into the phone. "We are holding hands".

Then we prayed. I distinctly heard the "Amen" from both of them after our short prayer. They agreed to come for counseling the next day. Before ending the conversation the man said, "Brother I need tolerance". Next day they came for a session. The three of us sat together on the floor of the counseling room. The man was not used to squatting but agreed to try and did sit down in a manner. Then he asked me, "why this insistence on sitting down on the floor?" I did not answer but I suspected the woman guessed the purpose. Sitting down on the floor, it appeared was a willing sacrifice on her part. The man sat because he was caught in a fix. He thought his refusal would have put him in a bad light. In the first three minutes of responding to me, they agreed they have problems in their marriage and it took another two minutes for them to agree that they want to do something about it. "That is why we have come", almost simultaneously they said. He had many complaints. His staff was not fast enough.

They take such a long time to finish even a minor job. At home his wife is so sloppy that it takes ages for her to make a cup of coffee. He likes tea. But since it takes even longer to make tea he now takes instant coffee as he puts it. He drives at break-neck speed even inside the town, according to the wife. He takes less than five minutes to eat his dinner and then he runs upstairs to his computer. He does not take a step at a time; it would be three or two at a time in climbing. He likes to watch TV but does not have the patience to sit through the silly advertisements. (Bless him for that!). Through the Broadband connection he sees Hollywood thrillers and horror films. He does not like being questioned even if he is watching porn. "I have no time to waste answering unreasonable questions. What is there to share about the office and the people there? She doesn't like my complaints about my office. So why waste time with her? What if I watch some clips I like?" Often he goes out by himself and has dinner in some hotels. They have never gone to eat out together. On occasions she goes out with her girl friends.

The man says, "She is like a snail in bed. I have wasted my life with her sloppy ways. She did not want a child in the first year and that was the end of our marriage eight years back. Oh yea, we go to church and that is why I did not talk about a separation so far". Last night the trouble started when he was while watching some slime. They both have been sleeping in separate rooms for 'donkey's years' as the lady put it. She said, "It was almost killing to hold his hands last night". For the first time, I could see some glaring emotion in her face which was closer to fury.

She was a faithful antithesis of the man, thoughtful, orderly, and almost disgustingly slow, with an air of gentle elegance. Her lipstick was applied with nano-precision, her attire was in immaculate taste that none would want to disturb the fall off her sari. Her purse had two buttons and a long strap. It was surprising that she agreed to sit down on the floor. That was suggestive of her willingness to do something about their situation.

She is willing to put up with his thoughtless hurry provided he will let her have her pace. Both of them are image conscious and have not spilled any of their beans.

Not even the parents of both of them have any clue of what is happening with their marriage other than vocally wondering why they are not planning a family, now that it is already eight years. The life of these people is a study in contradictions. Here is a person in an indecent hurry and full of loud complaints. His spouse is meticulously systematic with plenty of complaints kept deep within but now beginning to come out as desperate efforts to defeat him. In eight years he has only thought of ways to control her and make her comply with his 'faster' requirements. All the eight years she devoted to resist his 'repulsive' urges for the 'faster' and put him down as intolerable and unworthy. They now have jointly come to the conclusion that it is time to say adios.

Once they received grace to understand what they were doing to each other, they were willing to take responsibility to do something about it as they promised at the beginning of the session. They found out without mutual commitment they would never be able to build up their oneness that is essential in the making of a family. Then they also discovered commitment will not happen without unconditional acceptance of each other. It took a while for them to realize acceptance of another person does not happen just like that in a huff. They also learned love emerges out of unconditional acceptance and that is made possible only by the grace of God. They also understood validating each other is an important part in relating.

I asked them to sit quietly for a while enjoying the air they are breathing. They had a strange look subtly asking "How do you enjoy the air?" I beckoned them to be quiet and slowly take in the air through their nostril knowing the air gives life to them and enjoy what the air is doing to them in all the cells of their bodies. They tried it and seemed to be relaxed. Sitting cross-legged for all this time did not seem to bother them other than still wondering

Then we talked about the present moment and the joy inherent in the moment. They simply sat for a long time, relaxed and breathing in softly. I again asked them to hold hands. They did.

The long and short of it is, they came to realize that their marriage would be stabilized and survive only in the grace of our Lord. It is grace all the way. They said 'amen' to that, taking their own time. Sitting down on the floor seeing them closer to the floor did something to them, though it was not primarily intended for that. It is perhaps not strange we notice humility has something to do with the receiving of grace. Once we come to have grace it is infinitely easier to practice grace in relationships and to save a disintegrating marriage. Even faster than we comprehend! The grace of our Lord Jesus Christ is faster when the receiving end is open wide.

Meta-love-counseling goes even beyond the ordinary manner of Christian counseling. It is not a tiring interrogative or investigative session. Realizing the potential of gentle tolerance, peace and acceptance go a long way towards healing.

The counseling was early in 2018 while I was just getting out of the Multiple Myeloma which was diagnosed in 2016.

The couple now has a three year old sweet girl child.

Susan

From the many instances that stand out let me tell you about Susan, a 65-year-old mother of seven, and eleven grandchildren. She worked in a women's hostel practically all her life as cook and the defacto chief of the place. She reluctantly retired at the insistence of her elder son who was by then a successful businessman, a wholesale vegetable seller. Her husband was a non entity doing what was told. He used to sell vegetables from a cycle push cart and made enough money to get the household needs for the big family. On very rare festival days he would indulge in some alcohol and would sing the litany of his suffering with appropriate acerbic responses from the wife.

He was under strict orders from all not to drink on special days and make a mess of the day. But that was one order he was brave enough to break. It must be said to his credit that he made himself enjoy all festivals despite the verbal thrashing he would gladly take in the next day.

Then when the woman of the house retired and started a somewhat sedentary life according to her, the husband was never in evidence before midnight even on weekdays. Gradually they drifted apart and the man was shut off from the bedroom.

He invariably ended up on the couch all night. Susan began to spread the news that the old man had some illicit relationship. People who knew him immediately discounted it. That must have been the last thought in his mind. He was the happiest to be away from anything "female".

But Susan began to spread graphic stories about the woman and even created a character and a place. She later began to accuse him of having relations with several women. She refused to sleep in the same room with her husband even after her children pleaded with her. Sam too was afraid to be in the same room with her, because of her suspicion she started physically assaulting him threatening to cut his throat. It was a clear case of what psychiatrists would term as the "paranoid schizophrenic" patterns of behavior. It called for immediate and ongoing heavy medication. Susan was in no mood to be convinced that she suffered from paranoid schizophrenia. She was a perfectly balanced person in most other areas of thinking as is the case in all such patients. She would expertly pick up what was wrong with everyone else. In the course of our talks she would repeatedly ask me. "You understand?" She was quite sure I did not. About a week before her visit, according to her eldest son, she was keeping a hatchet under her pillow to kill any woman who might happen to be in their bedroom or home. That is when the family panicked and brought her for counseling.

There was nothing I could do for this person with advanced "schizophrenic paranoid" symptoms. She knew I was all attentive and she gave me an impression that she too was intently listening. All my training in psychotherapy starting with classical analysis to client-centered therapy including existential, cognitive, behavior stuff passed through my thoughts. Medication was clearly indicated and I did succeed in persuading her to see a Psychiatrist.

When she rose up to go I sat bent down in prayer and as a passing thought I said, “Nothing is beyond our God. Our very presence on earth is because of him” She looked at me perhaps for a minute or so. I put in “Susan, wait for Sam this evening. When he comes home, have your supper with him, hold his hands and let him sleep in your room”.

“Oh yes sir, that is some comfort”, she said while going out, with all the sarcasm she could manage. I was not sure what her expression in the eyes had when she said that. “You can be sure of it Susan. All things are possible because HE is in control”. I had to say that somewhat audibly as she was already out of the counseling room even without a goodbye.

I kept praying about Susan. Her son had promised to ring me and tell me the developments after a week. For almost ten days I had no news from them and being concerned I called the son and asked how things are. “Oh, oh, yes, yes, Mamma and Papa! They are alright. Thick friends now! Sorry, I forgot to call you. We are all so happy. Thank you. I will tell her you called”.

Obviously I did nothing precious to cause such a drastic change in a severely paranoid schizophrenic woman. I definitely ascribe it to the ‘BECAUSE’ and nothing else. There are some simple facts we tend to ignore due to its absurd simplicity. In meta-love-counseling these simple facts would be taken out to be almost miracles? That statement would call for a definition of a "miracle". We love to believe miracles happen when God performs unusual, benevolent things in accordance with the desires of man. The celebrations of such miracles and its heights would depend on how far it is from the ordinary. But the truth is miracles happen when men act in accordance with the purposes of God and do his will. It is not always exciting for all to wait on the Lord and seek his purposes and act in accordance with it. That would be giving up control. Lack of control is so frightening that we generally do all things possible to retain control. That is when miracles evaporate and leave a residue of disenchantment. If as a meta-love-counselor you want to see miracles happen in your counseling, you need to be prepared to move mountains.

Mark

The next instance can be put across in a few lines. A retired very senior officer, a woman of high power and profile from the army sent her 22 year old son to me escorted by a retired Subedar major who was her ADC; sort of. The young man was an 8th Semester Architect student in a prestigious institution in another State. This was in the first week of January. The boy had come for the Christmas holidays. Having nothing better to do than while away his time at home, he went to Velamkanni Matha shrine for a pilgrimage with a team going there from his church. He was there for three days and wanted to stay back. The tour manager could not agree to that because he has to bring him back to the place where he joined. The manager is responsible for the boy's safe return. After reaching back home he has the freedom to do what he wants. Back from the pilgrimage and even after his holidays he showed no signs of going back to college.

He is not communicating much but made it known to his mother that he wants to go back to the Shrine and wants to stay there permanently. No more of college. His mother was not frustrated, just fumed and hurled her baton at him. It hit him in the chest. His mother's shouting and hollering made no difference. She even beat him up with a belt. "I am not going back to college. I will live in Velamkanni from now on. You do what you want". His stand was final. That was the first time he dared to say that much to his regal mother.

His proposition is impractical and he is in the final semester of his engineering undergraduate course. During the course of counseling on the first day, the boy simply sat in the chair offered and did not respond to my greetings and did not seem to recognize my presence even. I sat with him cool and quietly praying and trying to maintain a pleasant smile. We sat there just like that for almost 45 minutes. He was observing me from the side of his eyes but with no eye contact at all. Then I slowly extended my hand and gently stroked his head. He abruptly raised his head and looked straight into my eyes with a deeply mellowed look and I felt a rush of love for him. That must have been obvious to him from my face and body and he gave me a mesmerizing smile. We sat like that for almost two minutes or so. Both of us did not know what to say.

Finally I got up and gave my hand to him in a warm handshake. He gripped my hand like a grizzly bear and asked when he should come next. I told him to come any day of his preference. "I will come tomorrow" he said eagerly and as he was going out he turned round and gave me a huge hug and held on to me for a few seconds.

He came the next morning fixing up a time at 10.00am. After warm greetings and with no invitation from my side he started telling me his situation. He has no memory of seeing his father. He died when Mark; that is his name, was just ten years old. Most of his life he lived with caretakers or in hostels. On holidays Mama would send for him if she is at the station. There never were many interactions other than instruction to do this or that. When it is time for him to go back to school, he has to stand before her like a statue and ask for money specifying the amount he wants. He waits for a while till she writes the check. She hands over the check to him and he vanishes from her sight.

I was not surprised at this as I had a similar experience with the son of a Brigadier. The only difference was that he went to Sabarimala.

When Mark was at Velamkanni, he was right in the middle of so many people. After a particular retreat many people came to him and embraced him. Some said 'Love you', 'Jesus loves you', 'Bless you', 'Praise the Lord', 'Be blessed' and a lot more of 'Love you'. "Shouldn't I go to a place where love is; love is accessible and available? Why should I be miserable before it is my time?"

He finished his story and waited for me to tell him something. After a few minutes I told him; "Let us enjoy this moment, the calm, the air, the light and the joy right in this moment". We did not know how much time we sat like that. Mark drifted into a restful nap. I touched the back of his arm gently and again more gently called him 'mone' (meaning 'son' in our language) and some wonder was evident in his face. Then he started sobbing and into unabashed weeping. It took some time for him to get back to normalcy. I found grace to tell him, "If you feel like weeping some more, no need to feel ashamed please do continue".

"This is the first time in my life I hear myself addressed as 'mon'. Where am I?"

He straightened up some seconds later and asked me "What do I do now?"

I said "You do not have to do anything. But whatever you think is right for you and for your future and your family will come to you" He became quiet and we sat there for another twenty minutes or so.

Finally he said "I have no family"

"Now?"

"Yes now; but you do have a life ahead".

"Yes I do, I trust I have". After another five minutes he got up to go and extended some currency notes to me.

I gently forbade him and said "Not now, from your first salary"

He started sobbing again and rushed in to embrace me tight and gentle.

Turning to the door several seconds later, he said "Bye uncle" and he was gone.

(I had a call three years back from him inviting me to his marriage. I could not go. Recently, I heard he is in Canada with his wife. They have an Architectural firm. His wife also is an Architect from VIT, Vellore, Tamil Nadu).

What are the factors that would negate the freely available benevolent grace to the healer in His stead? The list may be incomplete but let us begin with the first; its acts of miraculous benevolence

There should be no one in your life whom you have not forgiven. Forgiveness is the first in the list. There are many things which follow that we need to be mindful of; Remove all hatred, resentments, irritations, annoyances, broodings, anger, suspicions jealousy, cursing, vengeance, vendetta, harsh memories, manipulative measures, conspiring, evil motives; all generated internally.

Erase all blasphemous thoughts, doubts, miss-concepts, cowardice, pretensions, fear, ungodly learning, reliance on lucky talisman and holy threads, absolution on payments, touting god-men and god-women offering spurious blessings, superstitious sorceries, voodoos and the like.

These things should not upset you thinking how on earth can you achieve all this erasing and removal? There is no need to be unduly concerned, because all these are part of the grace of God given freely to those who live by faith. All these are simply part of the Grace that is our due in Him.

In Meta-love-counseling, it is not what you do or required to do is important. It is about who you are. Not doing; but being. I hope you get what I am trying to put across. Your ' BEING'! Counts

Be holy and be close to God with no malice, no anger, no jealousy, no guilt, no unforgiveness, no spite, no dishonesty, no pretensions, no covetousness, no vengeance, no bitterness, no sloth, no hatred, no boasting, no image building, no rhetorical lying, no histrionic performances, no assumptions, no judging, no partiality, no patronizing, no partnership with criminality, no addiction, no destruction, no manipulations, no calculations, no disrespect, no pride, no lying tongue, no two masters, no problem walking the second mile, no abuses, no hostility, no critical attitude, no avarice, no gluttony but with purity as pure can be. Purity and holiness in being are essential requirements. In all that you read above you do not have to do anything; just BE; giving up all that happens without your having to do anything. If these existential qualities have not happened within you already, make yourself available for the Love-Truth to make it happen. Here also you do not do anything. You just are available, as you are; open for the Love-Truth to be in charge.

The Meta-love- counselor role is to BE; simply present in the counseling situation as an actively blessing presence; a reflection of the Supreme Presence. The meta-love counselor is a blessing presence totally disposed to be a blessing, wholly aware of being there filled in boundless blessings and contagious joy. Meta-love-counselor totally engrossed in peace and conscious of the overflowing love is not eager to take control; being infinitely patient with no signs of any hurry. In Meta-love-counseling we keep away from intrusive investigative interrogative modes of interactions.

You are led in gentleness by the Holy Spirit and you in turn lead the counselee in your gentle healing presence in the fullness of the Love-Truth that abides in you through faith and ensuing grace. The healing restoration of the counselee does not depend on Meta-love-counselor but is of the meta-factor; the Holy Spirit of the Love-Truth using the meta-love-counselor as His tool.

PETAL-20

DIMENSIONS OF META-LOVE-COUNSELING

A question asks itself. What then is the extra dimension of Love-Truth and Meta-love-counseling? The disarming answer is that love-truth meta-love-counseling ushers in healing of the counselee with no manipulative moves from the counselor but totally in the divine provisions. The Love-truth- Meta-love-counselor merely functions as a vehicle or a conduit of healing with absolutely no pretensions. He simply eases and witnesses the marvel of healing being assured in faith of the unfolding miracle.

Meta-love-counseling stands out beyond the ordinary concept of 'Talk Therapy'. The Meta-love-counselor sees everyone as related and belonging to and being in God. No one is an island. The counselor cannot exist and operate as a separate, isolated entity. He belongs to all and is connected to all else, in and through God, the Omnipresent. That is the wonder of Meta Counseling. Neither darkness nor unbelief can separate the Meta-love-counselor from the people to whom he belongs to. The great principle of Meta-love-counseling is a mighty bond that connects you and me; all into one total Being.

If I for a moment believe that I am special and separate, I am doomed to wither and dry. A dry twig is of no use to anyone other than being a burst of heat in its burning. A dry twig falls off and sinks into ashy nothingness to be received in soil at best as manure. Life is in the joined existence of the One who is Love-Truth, Light and Life. Only the ones who are connected and related can see and interact meaningfully as one in each other.

Meta-love-counseling is holistic and synonymous with completeness which implies perfection. To get into the holistic mode for a deeper understanding of completeness a larger wider look would be needed. Let me try to put it differently. Human beings carry on life at least in four different levels or modes of existence.

The basic level is a self-centered one; subjective, which is asking oneself, what is there in this situation for me? Can I get something out of the present happenings? In short looking for personal benefit in any given situation.

The second level is a searching objective level looking for means to use the situation in turn for your own advantage. What in the present situation can I change for personal benefit? In essence it is an indirect subjective manner of looking out for possible personal gains.

The third level is analytical, intellectual inquiring for more information and seeing everything from all possible angles for a greater in-depth understanding of whatever may be happening. There may or may not be any profit motive behind the inquiry. Even here the center is the self.

The fourth level is what we could call as the non-personal existential level in which the person concerned exists for spreading benefits indiscriminately to all other beings; existing to bless others or for being a blessing in existential terms.

In the first three levels of existence above, there is obvious and implied search for self aggrandizing and self satisfaction. We may ask what is wrong with it, after all man exists for gaining benefits from his environment and to improve his life situation. That is fine as far as it goes. But if man tends to stop all searches to end in him, man does not move ahead of the self and is condemned to shrivel within. The subjective, objective and analytical type of existence miss the holistic content of existence and interpret life not based on truth. True wholeness of man can never be total without incorporating the spiritual content which is concerned in selfless giving and sharing. A dominantly spiritual being who dwells in the fourth level rejoices in sharing and finding purpose in existence.

When it comes to Meta-love-counseling any element of self concern would be counterproductive. We have said earlier that counseling is an act of love. All or any kind of counseling ought to be acts of love. Counseling done for gaining personal advantages of any description cannot be designated as a helping blessing process. That can only be designated a dented self seeking gain which is devoid of any cognitive awareness of truth. It goes against all healing professional mores and expectations to act in such a self-centered manner.

And in the final analysis counseling; IS AN ACT OF LOVE. I repeat, no Counseling takes place in an environment devoid of LOVE.

A Meta-love-counselor moves beyond the dichotomy of the physical and mental (mental = emotional + intellectual + volitional) to reach up to a spiritual blessing-mode-of-existence; in all relating including the counseling as acts of love. Holistic integration in counseling is not just linked to the physical, intellectual, emotional, political, social or any other self oriented activities. Meta-love-counseling is to be in harmony with all that coalesce with the existential order of 'Being'. It may be a bit hard to grasp; the long and short of it is, counseling as we envisage in the Meta-love-counseling context is totally in agreement with the fourth level of existence we mentioned above; that is simply concerned with being a blessing. The fourth level turns the entire perspective on counseling by transcending all the three other levels and lifting the process into a pure wholesome state of consciousness not around the self but on the whole of existence itself.

When we go on like this, it is a natural inclination to ask, what is it that we refer to as Existence? That question is relevant and needs addressing. Man exists and existence manifests itself as all aspects of the 'Being' of man. In a way, if I say man is a living entity manifesting existence, bearing witness to the whole which is not only man but everything living and nonliving; the whole, will that be closer to the truth?

The human consciousness only can truly lend itself into harmony with existence. It may not be happening as such for all practical purposes, yet the human consciousness is capable of constituting such a base for existential wholeness in love; let me add holiness, health, humility, truth and maturity. Yes or no? This is not meant to be a coercing style of a well advertised guru, to make people say 'yes'.

My purpose in leading you to this point is for you to realize that wholeness as we conceive in the context of man is a presence in the **Presence** of Love-Truth. This has a total bearing on what we try to understand as Meta-love-counseling. The counselor's blessing presence in Meta-love-counseling stands out as love, peace, joy, patience, kindness, goodness, faithfulness, humility, self-control, tolerance, beneficial and creative compassion, acceptance and all that is sublime in relating to God's provisions. The inherent resilience in 'agape' love wherein holiness reveals itself as a prerequisite comes alive in Meta-love-counseling. Therefore the very presence of the Meta-love-counselor lends him/her contribute to the wholeness of the counselee's all-round development and growth.

Speaking of the wholeness of man we have to concede that man has a trichotomous/ternary mode of existence, meaning the total man is made of three parts, the Body, Mind and Spirit. The mind itself has three parts in turn which are Emotions, Intelligence and Volition. While body, mind and spirit form one third each of the total personality, emotions, intelligence and volition form one third of one third each; that is one ninth. We can represent that in pictures:-

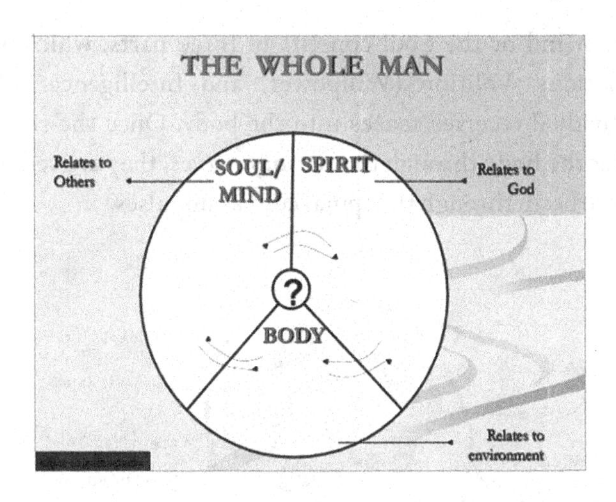

The trichotomous make up of man, Body, Mind (Soul) and Spirit.

Man is not aware of what he holds at the core of his being.

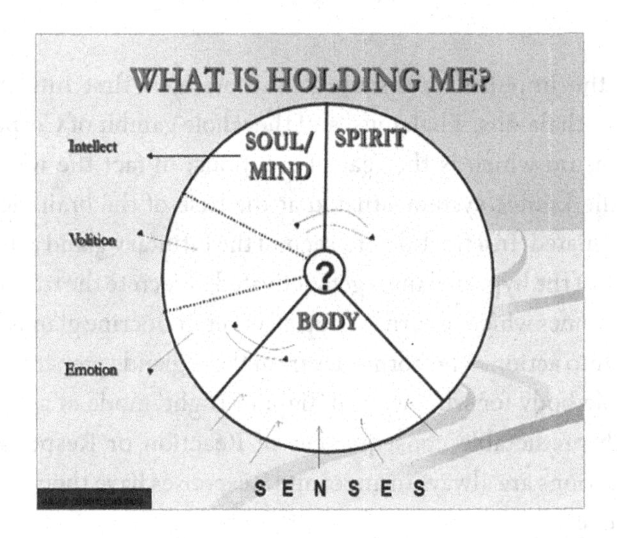

The Mind or the Soul consists of three parts, which are Emotions, Volition (Willpower) and Intelligence. The individual receives senses into the body. Once the senses enter the body through the sensory nerves, they are sent up to the brain through the spinal cord as impulses.

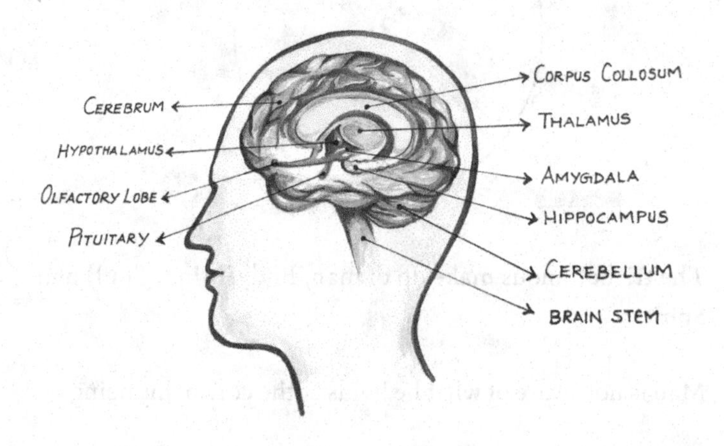

As the impulse travels up to the brain, it first hits the Hypothalamus, Thalamus, and the whole gambit of Corpus callosum which is the seat of emotions; in fact the whole of the Limbic system situated at the base of the brain gets stimulated. In a fraction of a second the Pituitary gland at the base of the hypothalamus gets activated to secrete the trophic hormones which in turn kick up all other Endocrine glands to get into action. The hormones from these glands prepare the whole body for what we call 'fight or flight' mode of action with predictable consequences of Reaction or Response. Reactions are always in anger and Responses have their base in love.

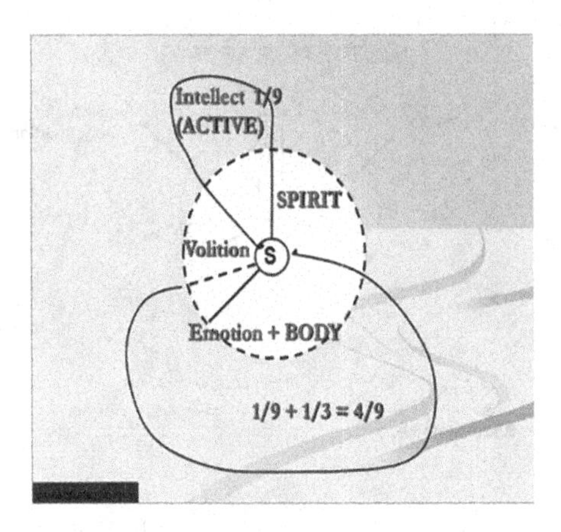

Once the endocrine secretions invade the body, the emotions and body get into an elevated level of activity; the two in fact become a powerful emotions + body combine which ignore the soft mumblings of the intellect. Momentary reactions result with hardly any intellectual inputs. If the individual has no spiritual resources to fall back on, all sorts of thoughtless acts ensue resulting in a distortion of the person-hood.

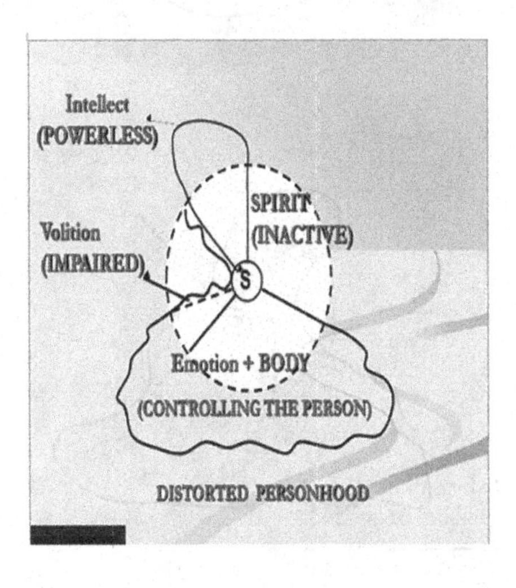

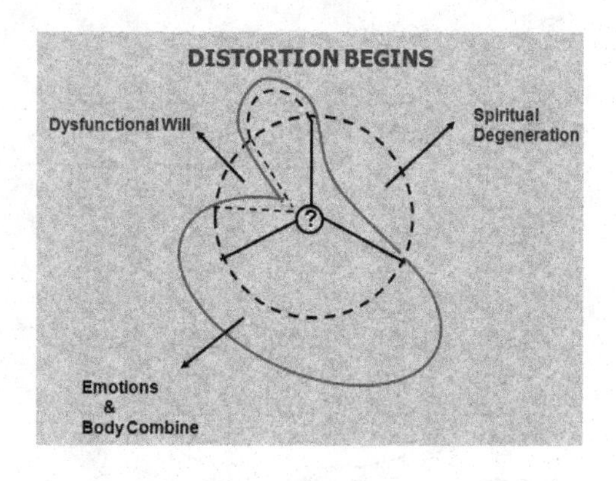
DISTORTION BEGINS
Dysfunctional Will
Spiritual
Degeneration
?
Emotions
&
Body Combine

EMBODIED EVIL

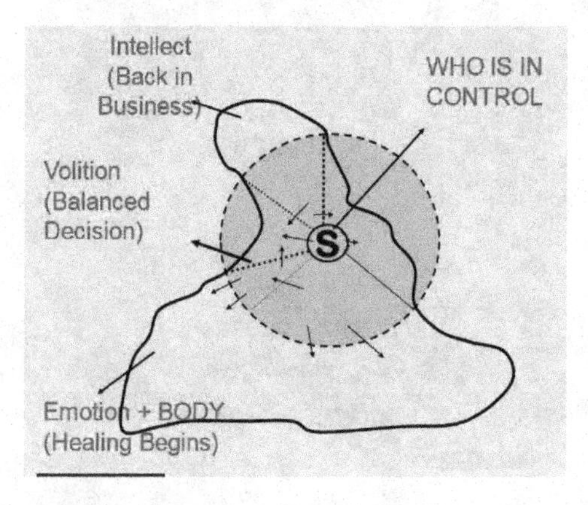
Intellect
(Back in
Business)
WHO IS IN
CONTROL
Volition
(Balanced
Decision)
S
Emotion + BODY
(Healing Begins)

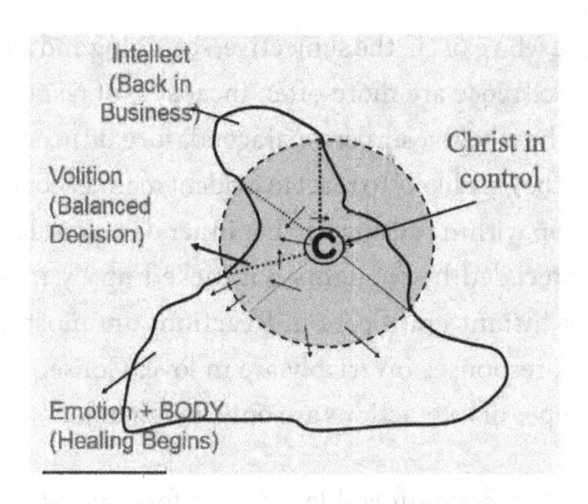

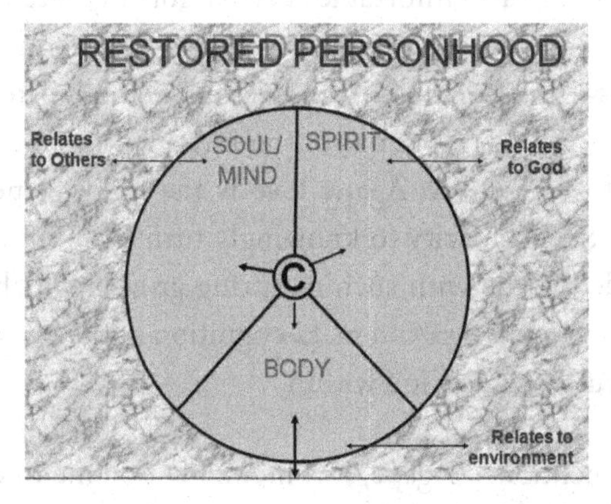

When personal distortion like these happen with the redoubtable self in the center of the personality, it has to be replaced by the blessing presence of Christ Jesus represented by the 'C' in the center of the last picture.

The degenerated personality will be restored by the Blessing Presence of Christ in the inner most core of the person of Christ in the center. That is total regeneration of the person.

He who knows Love-Truth knows how to respond lovingly in

life. Those who exist in the subjective, searching and analytical mode of existence are more often incapable of responding in Love-Truth as they have a personal agenda for gain in one form or another. They are likely to react in evident manners or suppress the reaction within causing further inner damages. Reactions are not preceded by thoughts but kicked up by instinctive drives for instant gratification. Reactions are most often in anger; but responses invariably are in love. Consequences in the two types of interactions are only imaginable.

Anger is not a comfortable answer for any situation in life whereas a loving response is the sign of maturity and godliness. Emotionally driven lives cannot be open for the revealing Love-Truth, vital in the imminent moment. The ability to respond in Agape love is the mark of personal growth. Such capacity to knowingly turn away from anger goes side by side with such maturing growth which is the underlying godliness and meta-cognition of the presence of Love-Truth, that is; God within.

Since I mentioned Agape, it is incumbent on me to explain what it stands for and that needs a comprehensively wider dealing of love as a whole.

The concept of wide love excludes nothing as unlovable which means, love all, everything, every living being, as from God, every non-living, in fact every being with or without life as we conceive it and beyond. All that keeps happening in Meta-love-counseling is totally based on inclusive love. The types of all-inclusive love; excluding nothing is a possibility. All-inclusive love to be practical and practicable has certain basic pre conditions. The foremost of which begins with: - Acceptance

Acceptance is based on the fact and belief that all things are given; all things are created and provided. Acceptance of all things can only be possible in a theistic frame of mind. An impersonal big bang purported to have constituted the foundation of all that is; at best a rationalization. Tracing the evolution of things and beings from pre-existing things are also in the intimate analysis a rationalization which maintains that it cannot be any other way and therefore it has to be as it appears and possible. Faith also is rationalization. We have the choice to choose the more valid rationalization depending on our value system and belief structure. Finding fault with each other does not come to a conclusive agreed understanding. The eternal question of who is right will remain unresolved creating wider gaps between those of us who are meant to be one. That being an impossibility, let's not waste time in a debate on it.

Having agreed or disagreed on the utter dimensions of 'wide', let us limit ourselves to the possibility of loving and knowing love in its wider sense.

Tentatively considering that wide includes all, shall we look into the possibility of loving all and everyone and everything widely?

> Is this concept an utopia or a practicable idea?
>
> It is practicable and practiced by at least by ONE that the world knows of.
>
> This person loves indiscriminately.
>
> This person loves everyone.

This person respects and honors everything

This person compelled by the visible, was not unwilling to call a spade, a spade.

That is; He had no hesitation in calling a spade, a spade.

He always acts in ways beneficial to all He interacts with; all whom He touches.

Redeem all and bless all was His manner of living while on earth.

Give to all, to the impossible extent.

His giving culminated in giving Himself, giving of Himself.

He kept giving and exhorted others to give as He gave and even as He gives.

His specific request or command is to love as He loves.

To give as He gives,

To serve as He serves.

To bless; as He blesses,

To forgive; as He forgives,

To share as He shares; in the sufferings of others.

He encouraged people to use their eyes.

To have eyes that see.

To have ears that hear.

To have hearts that love.

To have enough faith to move mountains.

To knock and keep knocking till an opening happens.

To seek and keep seeking, till you receive.

To have the dogged insistence till you are filled.

To keep asking till the impossible became possible.

He said and demonstrated nothing is impossible in love.

There are no problems big enough that cannot be solved in His love.

He told through His dear disciples that love can accomplish all things.

Through them and through object lessons
He taught the people that:

Love is patient

Love is kind

Love is gentle.

Love is humble

Love does not envy

Love does not boast

Love is not proud,

Love does not brag

Love is not rude,

Love is not self-seeking,

Love does not enjoy the failures in others

Love does not react in anger,

Love knows to respond only in love,

Love is not calculative.

Love does not manipulate for self-gain.

Love rejoices with truth.

Love is protective, goes out of the way to offer help

Love has no problem in trusting

Love keeps hope.

Love perseveres.

Love is resilient.

Love is not fiction.

Love is for real all around.

Love is Love-Truth in epistemological substance.

Love- Truth never fails.

Love-Truth finally wins all the time.

Love-Truth never fears or feels threatened.

Love-Truth is much more than all that is said about love.

Love-Truth never runs away abandoning love.

Love-Truth listens; have all the time to listen.

Love-Truth understands.

Love-Truth is ready to accept and help.

Love-Truth recognizes evil and is ready to forgive.

Love-Truth does not believe in condemning and destroying.

Love-Truth is bent on building up.

Love-Truth witnesses in its all-encompassing tolerance even of evil.

Love-Truth does not reject the underdog.

Love-Truth does not strut.

Love-Truth has fellowships with the lonely and rejected.

Love-Truth does not look into the history of anyone.

Love-Truth is ready to accept you and me as you and I are.

Love-Truth does not demand change prior to accepting any.

Love-Truth accepts the least and the lost.

Love-Truth's constituency is the marginalized and rejected.

Love-Truth brings in hope and expectancy even in the least.

Love-Truth has no problem in maintaining a hearty sincere smile emerging from within.

Love-Truth does not seek acceptance.

Love-Truth does not expect appreciation.

Love-Truth understands the volatility of appreciation and condemnation.

Love-Truth does its best; that is the end all and be all for love.

Love-Truth has no problem in embracing the unlovable.

Love-Truth considers no one as unlovable.

Love-Truth touches the untouchables.

Love-Truth does not believe in class structures.

Love-Truth is not into commercial profit practices.

Love-Truth cannot be contained by big impressive structures.

Love-Truth does not dwell in pilgrimage places or cathedrals.

Love-Truth leaves no relics or images to be worshiped.

Love-Truth does not desire exposure or show off.

Love-Truth is not a visible commodity in places of commercial transactions.

Love-Truth is always a given.

Love-Truth cannot be manufactured ever.

Love-Truth is not what is on sale in temples, mosques, churches, ashrams, and gurudwaras and so on.

Love-Truth visits you in person when you are lonely

Love-Truth visits you when you are upset.

Love-Truth feeds the hungry.

Love-Truth clothes the naked.

Love-Truth is not a by-product in meditation but a means.

Love-Truth grants the disposition to meditate on Love in Love-Truth.

Love-Truth makes itself manifest to the meditating soul without the soul being aware of it.

Love-Truth's transactions are always wholesome

Love-Truth is visible, audible, tactile, and sensitive to taste and smell, and sensible beyond senses, in oneness with Love itself.

Love-Truth offers life but expects no kickbacks.

Love-Truth creates awareness in the spirit of man in tune with the Holy Spirit.

Love-Truth cleanses; cleansing is easier in isolation of meditative; coming apart.

Love-Truth does not compensate the demanding.

Love-Truth always happens; never grasped; never enforced

Love-Truth never lends itself to enunciation.

Love-Truth only happens and love-making is a fake, a misnomer,.

Love-Truth happens in conducive, free and fully giving environs.

Love-Truth shall not be taken for granted.

Love-Truth is not a cheap marketable commodity.

Love-Truth is infused into one who is ready for receiving it.

Love-Truth impregnates perfect goodness in receptive hearts.

Love-Truth fills our cups to overflow.

Love-Truth precedes goodness and mercy.

Love-Truth is an abode for whoever welcomes Love-Truth.

Love-Truth receives, accepts, rejoices and understands burdens.

Love-Truth restores and gives rest for the burdened soul.

Love-Truth offers buoyancy for the dense sinking soul.

Love-Truth uplifts those who empty their burdens in love to Love-Truth

Love-Truth sees and accepts me exactly as I am with no conditions.

Love-Truth knows exactly what I stand in need of.

Love-Truth stands ready to accept any burdens.

Love-Truth accepts my burdens and offers me rest in return.

Love-Truth is just there in me to share love to all who stand in need of love.

Love-Truth wants me to be a messenger of love and a conduit for Love-Truth

Love-Truth sets me examples for sharing love as fully as I receive.

Love-Truth fills me more, more and more as I give away more and more.

Love-Truth includes involved suffering in the wake of receiving Love-Truth.

Love-Truth says accept pain and suffering in course of receiving, giving and sharing Love-Truth.

Love-Truth thus makes you grow in pain.

Love-Truth is a many splendored experience, as it is paining too.

Love-Truth's ultimate consummation is in giving, giving and more of giving.

Love-Truth; remain in truth of love and keep loving!

This list is tedious and you are ready to give up?

But we have touched only the tip only of the love-berg that is Love-Truth.

It is to this Love-Truth; Christian meta-love-counseling wants to initiate you to love widely. Let us look at love in its different garbs and varieties. There are at least eight major types of love practiced by man as we have seen in an earlier Chapter. The exact type of love we ought to get used to will depend on our dispositions, fantasies and desires. There are interconnections and overlapping in the different varieties for sure.

PETAL-21

META-LOVE-COUNSELING IS OPERATIONS OF LOVE

Read with this;1 John 4:8 which says, 'God is LOVE'. We know and acknowledge God is LOVE. His nature is to love. Love emanates from Him. He is the giver of love for those who seek love. His love is available for all. Receiving his love is not through some commendable acts. He loves all and spreads love equally to all even to those who are not aware of it. His love infuses everything. His love sustains everything. His love does not vanish because some are unaware or even may refuse it. Those who refuse His love do not lose it. He does not stop loving because some walk away from Him. Even if we shut out His love, He loves. The greatest quality of His love is that His love is unchanging. His love is not dependent on anything external including our stubborn refusal of it. If it were so, we would be in a position to control his acts. We cannot make God act in the way we want Him to act!

Whatever happens, God does not stop loving. As light comes from the sun so love comes from God. Sun is not the source of darkness. God is not the source of indifference. God is not vindictive. He does not punish us to get even with us. A vindictive God is the product of ordinary human imagination. God does not get reduced to suit the limitations of human reasoning. The father in the prodigal son tells us something of God and God's love[113] (Luke 15: 11-32). God's love is a covenant love. His love is unconditional. And His love is never liable to be canceled despite our erring. It needs endless repetition that no counseling happens in the absence of Love. In Love, healing, comforting and rejoicing happen.

Wisdom and wholesome growth take place through Love. Well-being is never experienced where Love is missing. Love is the effective antidote for 'unease' which is in fact 'dis' ease or simply sickness. It is the sick and those in unease or dis-ease who seek counseling and who need comforting. Christian meta-love-counselor; are you equipped and fitted in Love to counsel? Remember, there is underlying godliness and meta cognition of the presence of Love-Truth, that is; God within.

Spiritual 'Onement' with Jesus in Abiding;

A relaxed body and emptied mind is now ready to be open to receive the Lord Jesus who is ever waiting readily to enter into the person as and when he opens his heart. "Here I am! I stand at the door and knock. If anyone hears my voice and opens the door, I will come in and eat with him, and he with me"[114] (Rev. 3:20). Here; there are five things required of us:

1. See, 2. Hear, 3. Open, 4. Receive, 5. Respond.

This calls for seeing and then hearing leading to opening, receiving and responding. The finer senses are to be even more finely turned to clearly 'see', 'hear' and 'open'. To 'see' the unseen; to 'hear' the unheard; and to 'receive' what is given. The heart demands an openness enriched by a fine sensitivity. When the heart honestly thirsts for the Lord, He does not distance himself from us. He will cause us to praise His name. Responding is a choice which must happen in the grace of the Lord. It is grace all the way in all matters we chose to act according to the will of God and be restored.

There is one condition which we ought to remember as indicated in[115] Matthew 28:20, which says, "Surely, I am with you always". That is complete answer to draw upon His grace that is available at hand. These acts help to pave the way for Jesus to abide in the person and establish a tangible spiritual unity in the seeking person. It must be emphasized here though, that when it comes to counseling, some are given more special grace to be counselors as is the way with the Lord in endowments of gifts. We notice some are graciously gifted to be counselors in His special provisions; training and inclinations apart. Right through this, the fact remains an abiding relationship with the Lord is the substratum to operate from, in Christian meta-love-counseling.

Purpose and Priority;

I am the True Vine; Abide in Me and I in you; you are my branches; abide in me; bear much fruit; for apart from Me you can do nothing[116] (John 15:1-5).

The Creator, Provider, Sustainer God, through Him, by Him, for Him, in Him, through all things made, offers himself as a place for me; even for me, to live. For my abiding to have real meaning and lasting joy, I must know something in detail about the place I am going to occupy. If Jesus is what the Bible testifies as to who He is; then, I need not look for a better place to live in. Not that it makes any difference in the facts, but it will give me more confidence to go ahead.

None of us will buy a house or a plot of land to make a house without making proper searches and investigations about the property. So let us begin with some basic inquiries. Who is this person offering himself as a possible place for accommodating me? What manner of person is He? Know Him, the Savior and life giver of all that has life.

The Christian called out to be a servant–counselor has to have his credential in order that he might be found right for the calling. It is an established principle and an indisputable fact worth repeating, that Christian meta-love-counseling is not per se what the counselor does, but rather who he is in Christ. In other words the identity of the Christian counselor is more important in meta-love-counseling than his technological proficiency. Healing in Christian meta-love-counseling ensues from the healer, transferred to the wounded, through the ministry of the meta-love-counselor in the fullness of the Holy Spirit. I like to put it that the Christian meta-love-counselor ought to be a 'Christ-actualized' person and not just a 'self-actualized' individual in the Maslowian mold.

How Are You?

A meta-love-counselor needs to enjoy holistic health that means physically, mentally and spiritually fit and agile. The responsibilities of a meta-love-counselor involve prolonged observation, attending, building up a relationship, listening fully, understanding and making out the problem, walking along – if needed the extra mile –, help to make out the person's contribution in the problem, proffering alternatives in quietness of the Spirit, helping to initiate the needed actions verbalizing the least and then following through and so on. I made this long list to make you realize there is need to generate the time and patience needed in offering meaningful help. A person with physical disabilities will not be able to stand up to the severe demands of this ministry unless that person is in sturdy health. A meta-love-counselor has to answer calls to facilitate wholeness in people distorted in suffering, pain and brokenness due to faulty coping with life. That is the general idea though there are many other aspects to meta-love-counseling. Your Priority then is to find satisfying responses to the first question in Westminster Catechism: What is the chief end of man?

Answer: The chief end of man is to glorify God and to enjoy him forever.

This question is a reflection of the innate desire in all human beings to discern the basic purpose for living. We know for certain that God's highest purposes are to do with His people. It is basic for all God-loving people to bring their purposes in line with that of God's. We are then satisfied to concede that the generic purpose of life for man is to glorify God and the highest priority is to do His will. Specific purpose for individual life evolves and comes into sharp focus as each individual dwells and learns what is in store in the love and grace of the Lord Jesus.

In the Catechism style then comes the question, how do we do it?

The answer: By obeying and doing his commands.

Question: What is the chief command?

Answer: To love all men even as He loves us.

Our highest priority then turns out to be doing his will through loving his people that we may glorify God. We are never tired of saying that a pointed responsibility in the life of a Christian meta-love-counselor is to be of comfort to those in any sort of discomfort through sharing the comfort he himself receives from the God of all comfort. God our Father is the Father of all mercies and the mercies we receive are in evidence wherever we turn. The whole universe declares the glory of God. The sun that rises in the morning giving 99 percent of all available energy to man is the first example. The more intensely we come to know Him and draw closer to Him we get a larger glimpse of the infinite goodness of God in the innumerable unnoticed facets of life on earth.

The fact that you can hold this book and read and understand the content is no small thing. The grass, the trees, the green pigment that converts the incident energy to chemical energy, the precious proportion of the gasses in our air, the location and functions of organs and organelle in living bodies, the marvel of the machines and gadgets and the unnumbered wonders in every square nanometer declare in large fonts the greatness of God. It is all ours to have and cherish. The privilege of receiving all this from the God who is in control of all things is the basis of our joy.

Yet man tends to take and maintain control of his own life inevitably going against the natural order of things and God's purposes, creating sizable problems for himself, his fellow beings and the environment. The one serious purpose of the Christian meta counselor is also to help man who strives to be in control, to recognize the One who is really in control of all processes that sustain life and offer comfort even in the most trying human situations. This does not mean that a Christian meta counselor is a specially devolved species of humankind. We like to say and maintain every Christian is a counselor elected to do good[117] (2 Tim. 3:16, 17), as branches in the same True Vine. We owe it to each other to love and comfort.

However, our loving and comforting should not turn into ritualistic obligations; it is the wholehearted response to others in the love and comfort we keep receiving from the Father of all comfort. We keep repeating this as this forms the basic tenet of meta counseling and our specific mandate. Meaningful help can only be given when we know the nature and intensity of the situation of the person in pain and discern the direction and specific goal to pursue in counseling as such. I like to believe there is an elemental craving in all God-loving humans to discern the direction and goal in the grace of God. The craving for right direction in the human make-up is more than the generalized and fundamental desire for physical needs such as satiety, security, sex, power, possessions and so on. Once we are on the move in the right direction we can trust Him to lead us on.

What is the greater and more suitable vehicle than specifically taking upon us the onus of comforting people in any sort of trouble with the same comfort which we ourselves have received from the God of all comfort?[118] 2. Cor.1:3-4. It is simply receiving God's love and releasing it to the needy, the discouraged, the disillusioned, the wounded, and the broken. I am honestly not tired of repeating this one fact over and over and over. It is an undeniable eternal fact. It is the foundational rock of Christian meta-counseling.

1. The Christian meta counselor's purpose is to glorify God in all acts being a conduit of His comfort to all in need.
2. The Christian meta counselor's priority is to love and serve those in pain and brokenness as she/he enjoys the comfort she/he receives from the Comforter.
3. The Christian meta counselor's focus is centered on Christ the Healer per se.
4. The Christian meta counselor's strength is the observable infilling, indwelling Holy Spirit in her/him.
5. The Christian meta counselor's readiness to walk the extra mile is in the Love that constrains him.
6. The Christian meta counselor's effectiveness is his/her Abiding connectedness to the True Vine.
7. The Christian meta counselor's affirmation arises from the abiding Christ in him.

8. The Christian meta counselor's assurance is the rest received replacing burdens given over to Jesus.
9. The Christian meta counselor's goal is to magnify God in word and deed and in her/his whole being.
10. The Christian meta counselor's end is to enjoy God, doing His will forever and being used of Him.
11. The Christian counselor's Holiness in an indelible mark
12. The Christian counselor's personal purity distinguishes her/him from the ordinary.

Is your heart in tune with the twelve things mentioned above?

Is your heart set to enjoy him forever?

If so; Christian meta-love-counseling is for you, your purposeful priority.

PETAL-22

TAKING LESSONS FROM COUNSELING OF JESUS

Having had a look in the previous chapter at the qualities essential in a Christian-meta-love-counselor, the abiding life-meta-love- counselor should further ask a few more questions of himself: How did Jesus deal with people in need?

What is my model for reaching out and blessing others? What has Jesus exemplified in and through His interpersonal dealing, teaching and healing?

What was at the core of the counseling/blessing He offered to people? We ask a series of questions which may possibly cause some irritation or disquiet. It is because we lay primary emphasis on the personal qualities of the counselor, not what he does as a counselor. The meta-love-counselor needs to be sure of his/her standing in faith and reliance on the real Healer, Jesus Christ. To find answers for these questions we need to take a closer look at some of the personal encounters Jesus had with people. If we understand the principles Jesus laid down through these encounters and succeed in applying them in our meta-love-counseling, great blessings are bound to follow. We need to arrive there in terms of understanding and applying these examples in our counseling procedures. We follow His footsteps in taking up the ministry He has called us to shoulder.

Two hundred (10 x 2 x 10 = 200) helpful approaches to deal with people are given below. I would not claim these are all the approaches sufficient to counsel people in every conceivable situation. However, the Christian counselor has to learn the basic lessons of Christian meta-love-counseling from Jesus, observing the way Christ Jesus interacted with people. As you get to know Jesus more and more and search the manner of His dealing with people more keenly, you would receive greater insight and strength to deal with all situations in His provisions. Besides, the Holy Spirit is within you as your guide and helps. Many believers have some hesitation in accepting this happening in the normal course of events. I would not want to push this truth down anyone's gullet. Nevertheless, as a Christian carrying on the meta-love-counseling ministry, you will be surprised the way the Spirit slips by your side to accomplish a peace-filled transformation of events and people. The Spirit transcends. The Healer heals. The Comforter comforts. You will be used by the Lord for His glory, not for any personal agenda.

Study keenly the following ten instances and its handling by the Lord Jesus. These 200 ideas would form a basic 'skills' instruction manual. There are many more hidden in the Gospels for you to explore and discover. Learning of other interactions, of which there are many in the Gospels, will give you another 20 ideas each in the least. Add on to it as you learn from Him in your onward journey in the meta-love-counseling ministry.

Let us look at some of the selected instances in which Jesus related to individuals offering them healing wholeness.

1. Jesus heals a leper

The first instance that comes to mind is the healing of the leper recorded in all the synoptic gospels. This man sits by the way and calls out to Jesus, 'Lord if you are willing you can heal me'[119] (Matt 8:2). Jesus, moved with compassion, approaches the leper[120] (Mark 1:40). This leper must have been a sight. Before Alexander Fleming discovered penicillin, there was no known medication for bacterial infections. Leprosy chiefly affects the extremities causing lack of sensation. Being insensitive, when injuries are caused in these parts, such as limbs, ears, nose and so on, they usually do not become aware of it in time. The wounds fester and body parts begin to rot because of secondary infections. Oozing of pus inevitably produces a stench from the rotting human body. People keep away from lepers. Lepers did not have free access to public places in Biblical times. They were denied all human contacts. Leprosy then had a worse status than AIDS in our times. Even today in the 21st century most of us normally would not voluntarily touch a leper. Keep this in mind and look at what was the response of Jesus to the call of the leper.

i. Jesus, moved with interpathic compassion, heeded to the cry, reached out to the leper and touched him.

Instantly the leper was healed. Several finer nuances of counseling are discernible in this instance.

(Jesus touched the untouchable. A Christian meta-love-counselor is not an 'out-standing' Christian, as it were).

ii. He offered a touch first, even before he began a verbal interaction.

(Be an in-touch person).

iii. The voice of the least in society was given a compassionate heeding. (Never play deaf to a poignant cry).

iv. Jesus did not bother to ask many leading questions.

(You do not have to pulverize a mustard seed to make out it has a kernel).

v. He attended forthwith to the cry of a person in need.

(Do not replace compassion with smart moves to dig out more).

vi. No task is mean as no individual is without worth.

(The price of every life is the same, which is the shed blood of Jesus).

vii. A loving touch has healing in it.

(Do that to witness the amazing results).

viii. The great and revered teacher did not ignore the cry of a filthy, stinking leper.

(Do not play the high and mighty professional. The sick need of a helper-: YOU).

ix. Jesus not only healed him, but also went further and encouraged the leper to get back to mainstream.

(Offer ways and means for a decent rehabilitation back to life).

x. Jesus took a bold, unpopular step dealing with the leper.

(Do we really have the boldness to do the unpopular for good, if need be?).

2. Jesus heals an enemy's servant

In[122] Matthew 8:5, a Roman Centurion comes to the Lord and entreats Him saying; "Lord, my servant lies at home paralyzed and in terrible suffering". The response from Jesus is incomparable. "I will go and heal him". No preamble, nothing of the inquisitiveness that kills the cat. Jesus senses the faith only later. Even before that He expresses His readiness to heal, not taking into account the enemy army status of the officer. What mattered to Him was the faith of the man and the fact that a poor man was suffering somewhere far away. Jesus was moved to express unconstrained appreciation of an apparently unbelieving individual.

i. He does not refuse help to anyone who seeks help from Him.

   (If we do refuse help by any chance, that would be conceit, an unchristian attitude).

ii. He does not waste time to search the background.

   (This is a repeated theme with Jesus. Connect to the pain of the moment).

iii. The actuality and poignancy of the presented situation is not lost on Him.

   (One unknown man's pain was more important to Jesus than being at the head of a procession).

iv. Pushing back personal inconveniences He is ready to go any distance.

   (Personal inconvenience is a small price to pay for the immense blessing that can happen in interpathy through you to a needy person).

v. Jesus discerned the believing attitude of the person even before the man said it.

   (Never forget the fact that the real discerner/counselor is not you! The Holy Spirit in you is).

vi. Jesus evokes confidence in the seeking person through His interpathic oneness.

(Who you are in Jesus Christ makes the difference).

vii. For Jesus there is no discrimination. He treats friend and foe alike.

(There is no Indian, Pakistani, Nepali, Srilankan or Bangladeshi; but a person in pain!).

viii. He shows there is no classification called for in suffering.

(Pain has no color, creed or class).

ix. Jesus is not stingy with deserved appreciation.

(You stand to lose nothing, making a person feel good about him/her. Building up is a Christian vocation).

x. He does not waste an occasion to put in a timely bit of teaching.

(Teaching also is an important aspect of the counseling ministry).

3. Healing a paralytic carried by four men.

In[123] Mark.2:3-13, we read of the instance of Jesus healing the paralytic. It almost looks like there is practically no counseling taking place during this incident of healing. However, there is plenty for the potential Christian meta-love-counselor to learn from here.

Jesus said,[124] 'Son…' (v. 5). Sometimes people may be forced to enter into counseling by others closer to that person. Psychologists maintain that this sort of counseling is bound to be less successful. Is that really so in all cases? Nothing is impossible for God.

i. Jesus honors the faith of the people who brought the paralytic to Him.

   (Faith is contagious. Simply because someone had to push the person to get counseled does not mean that person is beyond help).

ii. Proactive faith is given due recognition.

   [Recognize faith and honor it wherever it is deserved).

iii. Here again no searching questions are asked.

   (Counseling is not an interrogation exercise).

iv. For Jesus history is of no great importance.

   (Past should be spelled DEAD. Bury on burn it before it pollutes and poisons the environment).

v. There is evidence to believe Jesus had a good searching look at the sick person in interpathy.

   ('Those who have eyes, let them see' is not to be an empty teaching. Use your meta-love-counselor's 'eyes' to 'see' and respond in interpathy).

vi. Jesus on keen observation sees the repentance and subsequent openness to receive restoration in the person.

(Interpathic observation is a keen art which requires taking in all the noticed details).

vii. The sick man made no visible move for receiving healing.

(Seeing the unseen is a special divine gift).

viii. The person's willingness combined with the faith of the friends to receive was sufficient reason for Jesus to offer healing.

(Discernment of a finer order is expected of a Christian meta-love-counselor).

ix. Jesus in a blessing interpathic manner responded to the repentance in the countenance of the paralyzed.

(Please remember, understanding not followed by a positive action amounts to a mockery).

x. A son-father relationship was offered to the paralytic.

(An interpathic, reassuring close relationship has miraculous healing potential).

4. Jesus pardons a sinful woman

[125]Luke 7:36-48 offers another set of guidelines for the Christian meta-love-counselor.

The Lord Jesus is an invited guest at the home of an important Jewish leader Simeon. A woman of disrepute comes uninvited and ministers to the Lord, cries her heart out, wets the feet of the Lord with her tears, wipes his feet with her hair, anoints the Lord with a prohibitively expensive perfume. Her ministry moved Him in interpathic compassion and not in puffed-up importance. None of this is to the liking of the Pharisees, and they murmur. This is the scene where the action takes place.

Moved by the callous contempt evidenced by the Pharisees the Lord Jesus, perhaps in pain and disgust, asks Simeon, 'Do you see this woman?' He is so sad they only look at her history and refuse to see her tears of repentance. Jesus interweaves in interpathy in this incident to make His point strike home.

i. An uninvited prostitute in the house of a big man told its own story.

   (Make sense out of the unsaid story).

ii. Jesus saw through the masks of the 'important' people.

   (Be wise to the fact that people have their own compulsions to pretend).

iii. Jesus' interpathic resonation to a heart broken in repentance.

(Do not allow your heart to become Furness-porcelain of a Pharisaic grain).

iv. He gave credence to her willingness to pay the price for past deeds.

(Recognize genuine repentance and give due credit to it).

v. Jesus gracefully received what a broken heart offered from its brokenness.

(Those who cannot receive gracefully are poor givers).

vi. He recognized and responded to the inner spiritual need in interpathy.

(Spiritual blindness is a serious handicap).

vii. Jesus did not take any effort to pull his rank with a person in brokenness.

(Counseling is not a regimented efficacious act).

viii. There was no attempt at 'history taking' to 'place' the person, as it were.

(History has lessons to teach, but all the same, in counseling, it is not more than a cadaver).

ix. Jesus did not hesitate to confront a hypocrite though the person was his host.

(Have your convictions sharpened never letting them get blunt in 'holier-than-thou' battering).

x. He did not miss an opportunity to teach a sound and relevant lesson.

(Live by your convictions. Deft use of illustrations is of great help. Use analogies and parables).

5. Offering responsibility to a hard nut

[126]Luke 5:27-30: Levi was a professional tax collector, not a soft man who would care for serving all and sundry. He did not fit in with the description of a 'gentleman'. Levi was in his den of vice working hard at ways to squeeze more out of the ordinary fellow citizens. The Lord recognized the potential in the person whom the society considered evil and rejected. Levi was not an improvement on Zacchaeus in[127] Luke 19, another despicable tax collector.

i. Jesus did not hesitate to take the initiative in reaching out to the rejected.

(It is the rejected who need the interpathic warmth of acceptance).

ii. He did not hesitate to identify with the despised, detested, rebuked, accused, scorned scum of the earth.

(The rejected are not looking for high and dry professionals; they crave for a human touch!).

iii. He let the reject know He was lovable and that He cared. (That sort of love acts as a catalyst).

iv. Jesus generated commitment in return for the loving care given to Levi. (Love's dividend is enormous, often beyond the imagination).

v. Jesus knew the apparently distant man was closer than many would have thought of.

(Make it a habit to keep your eyes 'open'. See the 'person' next to you in the bus or train, and minister love).

vi. Jesus took a proactive step to initiate a fellowship with the man. (Serendipity is a beautiful gift).

vii. He offered an invitation 'Come, I shall give you something constructive to do'.

(That is what he told you too. Was it not?)

viii. The action offered to Levi was something in which Jesus offered a partnership too.

(You are not just a spectator, be willing to be of support where needed).

ix. Jesus also knows workers for the kingdom do not materialize from thin air.

(Pleading helplessness is a lame excuse. 'Go therefore……..' is a commission,

[128]Matt 28:19-20).

x. Jesus let Levi know he was better than he thought he was. Levi never even in his wildest dream considered himself to be a worthy disciple of a great teacher.

(Validating a person is your obligation. It has tremendous dividends).

6. Jesus causes dramatic transformation

Another powerful counseling happens in[129] Luke 19:1-10.

Zacchaeus the odious little man, despised and scorned by the local population, desires to see the Lord Jesus as He passes. He never wanted an encounter. That was the last thing on his mind. Hiding was his big concern. The public would have spat upon Zacchaeus if he appeared alone in the open. Such was the reputation of the bloodsucker of a tax collector in those days. He knew it well and took all precaution to hide. He just hated a public appearance, yet yearned for acceptance.

Jesus hails him from right in the midst of the multitude of people and offers him a new status, which the man never imagined. The way Jesus engaged Zacchaeus made all the difference. Zacchaeus sensed love and acceptance in the eyes of the Lord Jesus. The change was dramatic, total and enduring.

i. Jesus spotted a guilty, hiding, curious, unusual person whom nobody else saw.....

(Keen observation is an important requirement in a meta-love-counselor).

ii. He identified the real need of the person in hiding.

(You are not a run-of-the-mill commercial counselor. You have the advantage of intuition and spiritual insights from above).

iii. Then He addressed the identified need with total sincerity.

(Delivering the pious line 'Be of good spirit' and walking away is not the ideal Christian response to defeated lives).

iv. Jesus offered an opportunity for the man in hiding to relate with Him.

(Offer social participation to the shy hiding person).

v. He simultaneously gave a lift to the sagging self-image of the self-decrying-individual.

(You as a person are very much a part of that offer).

vi. Jesus made the person comfortable doing away with direct confrontation of wrongdoing.

(Rebuke is a piercing arrow, never a garland).

vii. He gave an opportunity for the person to change in the warmth of loving care.

(Warmth allows bending; freezing only promotes brittleness).

viii. 'I am willing to risk my status for your sake' is a definite healing mantra.

('I am with you in this' lends tremendous strength to overcome).

ix. Jesus did not go by any laid down formula for measured, explicit change.

(Christian-meta-love- counseling is not a regimented game; it is a down-pouring of grace from above).

x. He openly expressed commitment for an erring, hiding person producing a wonderful result.

(If you are a saved person, you would know the power of that expression).

7. The lady at the well empowered to new heights

[130]John 4:7-29 is the incredible story of a woman of questionable reputation turning an evangelist.

A woman who comes out of her house in the heat of the midday sun to draw water (in the then prevailing social practices) tells its own dark story. Here again the Lord has no problem about risking His reputation. Helping the person out of her sinful way of life is His concern not what would happen to His reputation. Jesus is willing to go to any length to bring wholeness in one's life. He proves to be the Good Shepherd willing to forgo all personal discomforts in seeking and recovering the missing one.

i. Jesus begins with empowering the ordinary sinner.

   ('Give me water to drink' suddenly elevates the common sinner to a locus of power).

ii. He has no qualms about receiving a drink from an untouchable.

   (Jesus had no problem in lowering Himself to a position of a person in need).

iii. 'Touch the untouchable' is a lesson He teaches repeatedly.

   (A Christian has no excuse not to touch the untouchables. Who else should blaze that path?)

iv. Jesus always identified Himself with the marginalized.

   (The constituency of the Christian is the marginalized. The Christian-meta-love- counselor is bound to emulate his Lord and Master).

v. He gave an opportunity for the troubled person to talk about that person's convictions.

(The counselor is expected to elicit responses without killing the initiative).

vi. Jesus used the insight gained in the interaction for effectively presenting a challenge.

(The person in trouble is not aware where that person is going wrong. The meta-love-counselor has to act as an 'eye opener').

vii. He knew the difference between a positive challenge and a wasting argument.

(In counseling, there is never room for arguments. The counselor is expected to be good in the art of 'dialogue').

viii. The woman was convinced who she was talking to, who really Jesus 'is'.

(The reliability of a meta-love-counselor is vital in generating convictions in the person. The counselee also is bound to assess the counselor).

ix. The words and acts of Jesus were congruent and in keeping with His revealed identity.

(A Christian-meta-love- counselor's integrity should be beyond doubts).

x. Jesus instilled hope and assurance through His interactions.

(A meta-love-counselor's vocabulary needs to be positive, assuring the certainty of God's grace that is freely available).

8. Jesus, the great listener and educator

[131]Luke 24:13-35: The resurrected Jesus walks with two disciples on the road to Emmaus in this incident. He could have spared the trouble to walk all the way to Emmaus. This may not seem to be a great counseling situation. Jesus turns every situation to bless those with whom He interacts. Here there are a number of sound lessons for the prospective Christian-met-love- counselor to learn from this encounter.

i. Jesus listened with rapt attention to all that the disciples had to say.

   (Total listening is the major skill that a meta-love-counselor has to employ in the ministry. If you do not have time, please do not start the walk).

ii. Jesus walks the whole distance with the disciples, giving His whole attention to them.

   (Walking the extra mile is a distinct Christian virtue).

iii. Jesus made no attempt to interrupt until they ended their narration.

(The counselee must have the freedom to uninterrupted narration).

iv. There was no showing-off from Jesus.

(Pretension of any sort is uncalled for in a Christ-centered helping ministry).

v. Jesus did not come up with instant ready-made formula solutions.

(The meta-love-counselor should be wise enough to recognize when an educational session is called for).

vi. He corrected the inaccuracies in their narration not fearing their disapproval.

(Deal from a premise of adequate information and be unafraid of disapproval).

vii. Jesus was flexible in His schedule and went all the way with them.

(Rigidity is not particularly a Christian virtue that perhaps may be the commercial line).

viii. Once the goal was achieved Jesus did not hang around for a remuneration of any type.

(Freely have you received; freely give – always!)

ix. He did not forget to pray with them.

(That is the whole and singularly superior weapon the Christian has).

x. He shared what was offered and let behind a sense of warm awe.

(A Christian-Meta-love- counselor is to be a channel of peace evoking wonder).

9. Jesus is not averse to confrontation where it is called for

[132]Matthew 19:16-32: This is the incident of Jesus dealing with the rich young man with a perfectionist bend of mind. We get all sorts of people coming for counseling. Everyone has to be dealt with in a specifically applicable manner. Angularity of character and attitudes takes on endless varieties. The meta-love- counselor has to have the wisdom to deal with specific cases in an appropriate manner to be effective. This rich young man goes away with sadness in him. He must have been stirred enough to think at length about his condition.

i. Jesus was dealing with a man who wanted to know 'What shall I do to secure eternal life?'

(There are many who run about seeking to beef up the self. Self-esteem is the big crowd puller in town!).

ii. Here is an "I" centered person!

(You have a problem on your hands helping self-sufficient individuals).

iii. Despite the man's self-assurance, he had a heart to know the way to eternal life.

(Words are not always a true indicator of intentions; here interpathic discerning is called for.)

iv. Was this person testing the Lord to know the real depth of His wisdom?

(You never know; you may be on the testing stone before your counselee).

v. The rich young man, though no one could do better than what he was already doing.

(Size up the counselee and his unexpressed thoughts and intentions. This is where you count on your special advantage of the Holy Spirit as your own counselor).

vi. The rich person might have been out to get an OK from Jesus for His ways of dealing with life issues.

(Do not be quick to go out of your way to please a counselee).

vii. Here is a person who is an ardent adherent of the 'Karma' philosophy, 'What shall I DO?'

(This person is not going to be satisfied with anything less than doing something to get what he demands. Self-reliance is an ordinary trap that a whole lot of people fall into).

viii. This man keeps others out of his life other than for getting information.

(This is the IT age. 'Tell me what to do. I can take care of the rest'. Good line of approach! However, there is nothing much you can do as a meta-love-counselor with this self-complacent person).

ix. The solution Jesus offered to the man was far from the expected. It was not a less than stern confrontation, which leaves the man disappointed.

(You do not function as a 'restaurant waiter', delivering the order in exact terms).

x. The man goes away as a sad person.

(Do not expect an immediate and 100 percent success in all counseling you do).

10. Jesus was not hesitant to turn servant

We are on to[133] John 13 and the Last Supper in the upper room. The night before the crucifixion, He hurriedly calls together His disciples for a last meal and with the specific purpose of giving them an object lesson in servant-hood. He keeps aside His outer cloak, which signifies His leadership status. He washes their feet despite some protests and so on. After the act of a menial service He pointedly asks 'Do you know what I have done to you'[134] (v.12). When no answer was forthcoming He himself said 'I have left an example for you'[135] (v 15). Then He adds in[136] (v 17) 'If you know this and do this you will be blessed'.

If we hope for any blessing in the ministry of counseling we are called for, let us be ready to stoop down and wash the feet. If we miss His humility, we miss the whole point.

i. Jesus stoops down knowing full well who He is!

   (Do we know who we are? Who are we in Christ Jesus? Do we have a problem in giving up no our 'counselor' status?)

ii. At the core of His action is the perfect knowledge of who He is and what His mission is!

   (The Christian-meta-love- counselor needs to be sure of his/her identity in Christ. She/he also needs to be sure of her/his calling).

iii. Jesus had total self-acceptance and assurance that allowed Him to bend down before His own disciples.

   (A person without self-acceptance would feel threatened to allow himself to turn still smaller).

iv. The Lord used an object demonstration of a great principle for better appreciation by His disciples.

   (Be innovative in providing visual demonstrable examples).

v. 'Do you know what I have done to you?' is a pointed question to the Christian meta-love-counselor.

(Do all things in your counseling with total understanding of the purposes of Jesus in your life of service).

vi. The Last Supper was a type of group therapy extending the lesson powerfully to all participants.

(Be appropriately selective in choosing the right counseling approaches, as Jesus did).

vii. The Last Supper is evidence of the great love Jesus had for His disciples.

(Those who dare to love only can dare to humble themselves, a concomitant to following Christ Jesus).

viii. Jesus did no calculation in reducing Himself to the level of a menial servant.

(There is no room for calculations in love. Love never happens through calculations. A calculating person can never be open to love).

ix. A disciple would miss participation with his Master if he refuses to understand the Master's purposes for him

(A meta-love-counselor is one who is willing to be washed and cleansed by His Lord and Master).

x. Jesus shows through this incident that all counseling and all service transpire in an atmosphere of love-induced humility.

(The fact that no counseling ever takes place in an atmosphere devoid of love is brought home again here).

Whatever Jesus did He based solidly on the fact that He and the Father are one. He came to do the will of His Father. The Father is His strength. That source of His strength is invested in us who are willing to do the will of the Father through Him: "Believe me: I am in my Father and my Father is in me. If you can't believe that, believe what you see – these works. The person who trusts me will not only do what I'm doing but even greater things, because I, on my way to the Father, am giving you the same work to do that I've been doing. You can count on it. From now on, whatever you request along the lines of who I am and what I am doing, I'll do it. That's how the Father will be seen for who He is in the Son. I mean it. Whatever you request in this way, I'll do" (John 14:11-14, (The Message).

Most of all, love each other as if your life depends on it. Love makes up for practically anything in Jesus; the Source of All Healing … … and by His wounds we are healed[137](Isa 53:5).

"I will heal my people and will let them enjoy abundant peace… …"[138] (Jer.33:6) He sent forth His word and healed them[139] (Ps. 107:20). Jesus gave us a mandate to heal: "The Kingdom of Heaven is near. Heal the sick, raise the dead….."[140] (Matt 10:7).

"Freely you have received, freely give"[141] (Matt 10:8).

And all who touched Him were healed[142] (Matt 14:36).

Large crowds followed him, and he healed them there[143] (Matt 19:2).

A contact with Him is sufficient for healing of all sickness, including emotional imbalances. Following Him is one way of receiving healing. A meta-love-counselor must be a healed person to be qualified to heal. We need to hear from the Lord 'your faith has healed you'[144] (Mark 5:34, 10:52; Luke. 8:48, 18:42).

Having freely received healing, wholeness and comfort in Christ Jesus, the meta-love-counselor has to doubly ensure that he handles the calling and responds with responsibility and accountability to the provider God. Nothing can be taken casually as routine work in a government or corporate office or worse, as business dealing.

Qualities in isolation would not make an efficient helpful counselor. The meta-love-counselor needs to have a sound knowledge of the ways in which outside elements influence and corrupt the mind in every situation. The ways of men under pressure take them in the wrong directions that end up at the wrong bends. Some counselors encourage counselees to think through, see, and examine everything for insight on the assumption that the insight gained will make them free from all their problems. That is Gnostic thinking. The Christian-Meta-love- counselors should know that we are freed from problems in the grace of the Lord Jesus Christ. Therefore, it is also important to register the truth that there is only one right way to handle problems and that is; He knows the Way. He is the Way. He is the Truth. He is Life and He is Love.

The Meta-love-counselor must also discern the nature of specific problems blown up and compounded. He must also have the wisdom to understand the real needs of the person in trouble. Many counselors are confused by the expressed desire for the missing comfort. The maneuvers to sidestep the painful growing process to attain instant comfort are common human weaknesses. The counselor should not fall for the urgent prodding for quick gratification of desires. We cannot ignore the truth that the present experience has a purpose in the Divine provisions. The Christian meta-love-counselor has the responsibility to teach every sufferer the ability to interpret the present occurrences. This is where the issue of faith comes in, even if the counselee is not a believer in Christ Jesus. The expressed discomforts and miseries may only constitute apparent symptoms. The real problems are likely to be deeper and remain concealed to an untrained eye.

When anyone looks at the total or present experience from a frame of knowledge crowded in by emotions, what emerges is a confused picture. Emotions blind the person to truth because of the present pain and experience of grief. Nothing beyond the present situation would be seen. It is a working faith that enables one to look beyond the present and see a purpose of a loving God behind each experience. Each experience has something or the other to teach us. This is not a platitude aimed at superficial consolation. No experience is a waste in the Divine economy. If I believe that the whole purpose of my life here on earth is to glorify God, then I would have no problem in seeing beyond the present experience. What I am suggesting here is that the meta-love-counselor should have a sturdy belief system that enables her/him to see beyond the apparent reality of the moment. Behind everything that is apparent, there is the indelible truth that pauses at the throne of grace. The counselee need not contribute to this belief in the counselor. However, without this functional faith in the meta-love-counselor she/he will not be able to give direction to the counseling at hand. The m-l-counselor is searching for the truth behind the present experience of the counselee that she/he may gently reveal to the counselee in loving relating. The counselee will be disposed to accept this revelation from the counselor provided the counselee has already extended acceptance to the counselor. You may understand the importance of our position that counseling is not just what the meta-love-counselor does. Who she/he is matters in counseling. The credibility of the Christian Meta-love- counselor is her/his identity in Christ, more than the academic qualifications, expertise and facility with people – fixing techniques.

The M-l- counselor should be adept at the art of waiting on the Lord for the revelation of the truth of every m-l-counseling situation. This is the doing of the Holy Spirit through intuition, from the Scripture, and in any way He chooses to do it. When we say the Holy Spirit is the true counselor, it is not just empty rhetoric.

That is the fact of the matter.

Finally, he must possess qualities of gentle loving persuasion to enable the troubled person to take the first tentative step forward faith and healing through understanding the experiences in the light of a firm belief system.

All these qualities are available to the Christian who is familiar with and abides in the Word of God. An effective channel of the love of Jesus needs to abide in His Love as well as in His Word. Such a channel has the mind of Christ. A Christian meta-love-counselor abiding in His love knows to seek guidance in line with the purposes of God. He then receives all that he asks for in the infinite mercy of the all-giving God. The Bible is the tool that is available to make oneself fit for a healing ministry, and a Christian Meta-love-counselor has these resources in her/his Lord and Master. However, the m-l- counselor must have the skill to use the resources for blessing those in need of freedom from and victory over problems such as: failure, defeat, suffering, desperation, disillusion, guilt, confusion, pain, brokenness, hopelessness, etc. Skill does not proceed from papers blackened with ink; it proceeds from minds that are open to reach out to the needy, attitudes disciplined in the instruction of the Scripture and hearts that are constrained by the love of Christ. Let me repeat, the position of this book is that the Christian-meta-counselor needs to have Christ- like qualities to be an effective channel to deliver healing and wholeness in the counselee. With this in mind, some points are detailed below for the aspiring counselor.

PETAL-23

LOVE IN ACTION, LOVE MAKES IT HAPPEN

1. One with Jesus and His presence

As an act of love, the whole process of Christian-meta-love-counseling takes place in the mediation of Jesus Christ, the embodied love and in the strength of the Holy Spirit. Any positive movement towards healing has to take place in an environment of love and only in it. Even as one is paying attention and taking in all the bits of information, the right inferences are to be arrived at as to the nature of the person's problem. It is not much of an intellectual activity. It is more of intuition in the leading of the Holy Spirit. Intuition is knowledge plus active pulsating faith.

This is a very slippery area. Immature and ill-taught counselors, without the infilling presence of the Holy Spirit would tend to confuse their thinking and claim doing the bidding of the Holy Spirit. Anyone who has the assumed claim to personal excellence in technological cures is not likely to have the humility essential for receiving the guidance of the Holy Spirit. Only a humble and holy person would have access to the counsel of the Holy Spirit to be of help to those in trouble. In every instance of m-l-counseling that Jesus did what mattered was the person of Jesus Christ, the fact of who He was. That is true in every instance of m-l- counseling that His disciples do here on earth on His behalf being at least a feeble reflection of the immensely glorious presence of the Lord Jesus

It is who the –Meta-love-counselor is in Christ that makes all the difference in any sort of counseling and not very much what the counselor does. We stress this point repeatedly, because that is the disarming truth about Christian meta-love-counseling which is not some technological fixing. It is not expertise in the discipline of counseling but the experiencing of the depth of Christ Jesus which accomplishes blessed results. For both the counselor and the counselee in every m-l-counseling situation this brings about healing and wholeness. Sense the infilling presence of Christ, feel the healing touch of Christ, be drenched in the overflow of His love as the m-l-counseling progresses.

With Christ Jesus abiding in the meta-love-counselor and the love, joy, peace, patience, kindness, goodness, faithfulness, gentleness, humility, tolerance and self-control reflected in those persons, the counselee is moved to self-discovery of a kind that ushers in healing of unexplainable dimensions. A person who would have ended up as a dry twig is being received back into the Body of Christ. He receives all the life-giving nourishments, renewed life and continued growth. In Christian counseling an abiding relationship with Christ, leading the person into healing and wholeness is the ultimate goal.

Be a Meta-love-counselor who abides in Jesus Christ as His branch.

2. Be the salt and light you are expected to be.

Jesus Christ intends His followers to be preservers and healers in the society. As salt, they help to lead the people in suffering with a healing covenant with the healer God. Salt is an integral part of divine covenant[145] (Lev 2:13 and 2 Chron.13:5). More than that the m-l-counselor lends flavor to the insipid lives of the defeated and broken people. Being salt emphasizes the need for the m-l-counselor to be pure, white as pure salt in heart, to be an agent that purifies the stained, troubled hearts. Saltiness is of more importance in healing. A meta-love-counselor who has the preserving functions as salt helps to lend flavor to the failing tottering lives. A meta-love-counselor who is one with the Lord Jesus Christ has the privilege to be the light of the world. "You are the light of the world. A city on a hill cannot be hidden. Neither do people light a lamp and put it under a bowl. Instead, they put it on its stand, and it gives light to everyone in the house. In the same way, let your light shine before men, that they may see your good deeds and praise your Father in heaven"[146] (Matt 5:14-16).

He calls His followers to be light and much more as those who are representing Him in the ministry of positive enlightening of those in darkness. A meta-love-counselor is a person who has received the light and who lives as one giving light to the confused and erring people groping in darkness. Having gained a sense of oneness with the suffering person and already in an abiding oneness with the Lord Jesus, a Christian meta-love-counselor is in an enviable position to radiate light in the dark areas of confusion, misunderstanding, mismanagement and misdirection in the person in problems. Being salt and light, in the context of our understanding of Christian m-l- counseling, does a great deal in enabling the counselee to come to grips with the realities of life.

What a meta-love-counselor is in that understanding assumes even greater importance than what a counselor does by way of counseling. One should never lose sight of this very significant aspect of m-l-counseling that earns respect and trust. One should also clearly assure the troubled person that all the details of his problems will safely and confidentially be kept by the counselor. The role of light in counseling is not to broadcast the confidential details of the counselee's burdened life to the public eye. Be the right person to be a meta-love-counselor representing Christ.

3. See the person as that person really is.

A Christian needs to have eyes that really see the person with all his inner turmoil. Love, as far as human perception entertains it, may be blind. However, it is sensitive to what goes on around. Jesus insists that we use our eyes to see fully. We may look on for ages and fail or refuse to see. A Christian-meta-love-counselor cannot afford to be blind to the person's disorders. When we come across a person in need, please make it a point to take seriously the question that the Lord Jesus was constrained to ask Simeon at the banquet in his home[147] (Luke 7:44). Pointing to the woman who cried her heart out and wet his feet with her tears, the Lord asked the host, *'Simon, Do you see this woman?'* (Emphasis added).

We have the knack to see the irrelevant and ignore the important. Not all the people present there saw the heart-rending tears of the woman. All present at the party saw only her history and impudence according to their point of view. The Lord denies that luxury to the Christian-meta-love-counselor by implication. So let us look to see and really see the person in need before us. What does it take to 'see' really?

A simple answer is one should not be blind! One should be open to the present realities observable in the person. A keen observer is sensitive, unbiased, uncritical, nonjudgmental and true unto oneself. A person who is not whole perceives distortions in others. We stipulate abiding holiness as the essential first quality for the Meta-love-counselor because wholeness cannot happen in the absence of holiness.

Dealing with people, their problems and their lives, is not a casual commercial dupery. Men and women are fearfully and wonderfully made in God's image. They are not to be attended to with casual indifference.

Look to see the concealed divine image blurred by sin. Look to see the butterfly concealed in the caterpillar. Look to see the saint in the sinner. See clear enough to sift the sin and really see the hapless sinner apart from sin. Seen thus, a sinner entails love. Love the sinner as a basic condition to get on with the further stages of Christian-meta-love-counseling. Be a person with eyes that see.

4. See and hear the problem as it really is.

The human predicament in the confusing wilderness of life is a common factor in every individual. No one is exempt from it. All have sinned and fallen short of the glory of God. However, it is necessary to discern the specific nature of the problem the individual is experiencing to be able to render meaningful help. It is an established fact that most of the non-organic and even some organic 'dis-eases' are caused by wrong reactions to life situations. This means the Meta-love-counselor has to see and hear clearly to know well, those life situations of the individual and the individual's specific patterns of reactions to those situations. Seeing and hearing simultaneously call for diligently attending to the person.

Diligently attending to get a clear picture of the whole individual and that individual's reactions to life appears as an exclusive art. It is not an easy proposition to be able to 'see' and hear totally to get the entire picture. Without total hearing and wholesome seeing the Meta-love-counselor would be far removed from the experiences of the individual. The meta-love-counselor then would end up having only a blurred picture at best and thoroughly distorted one at worst. The hallmark of a totally seeing, hearing person is a person with a heart in a restful state. A person at rest is the one who resolutely practices giving up burdens to Jesus who promises rest in return. It does not take much imagination to know that person is a regular praying person.

Prayer is neither an art nor a science form. It is not a ritual nor is it a custom. There is no orthodoxy or unorthodoxy in it. It is neither modern nor ancient. It is a commitment by man to the present movement of oneness between man and the moment with God formatting itself to the glory of God.

Prayer is prayer, is prayer.

At this point, let me make a digression. Counseling is not a science nor is psychology, which is sadly mistaken as the root discipline of counseling. Love is the root discipline of counseling. Nothing else can be a basis for Meta-love-counseling as a Christian sees it. If a Christian is emulating his Master and Lord in ministering to the broken and marginalized then there is no other reference point in the meta-love-counseling. Seeing and hearing is wholly facilitated in an environment of love only, where Jesus is present!

He is Love.

Be a person with eyes that see and ears that hear.

5. Paying attention

Paying attention is almost a solemn, inviolably devotional procedure. If not, a counselor would be mocking the humanity of the person he listens to. In fact, by mere thoughtless human reactions we mock people, perhaps unintentionally. When a person in suffering painfully narrates his experiences, the counselor has to receive it fully. The reality perceived and presented by the person may be far removed from the truth of that person's situation. To discern the truth, the m-l-counselor must attend fully to what the person is trying to express through words and otherwise. That calls for paying attention fully, totally. Paying attention is more than listening. When there are things troubling a person that are beyond words, then words become a decrepit vehicle to convey the trouble. What is inside then is revealed in a different manner through different parts of the being, too. Here I do not refer simply to body language, as it were. There is a dimension to expressions beyond the parameters of the body.

'Non-verbal' may contain that dimension, yet not all of it. A Meta-love-counselor has to take in the entire information even beyond the visible, audible expressions to sense the meaning of it all. Partial or faulty attention will give a blurred picture which will consequently cause damage to the troubled person.

One must learn to purge private thoughts and concerns before and even as attending is in progress. It takes disciplined purging of all the mental loads that a m-l-counselor carries about. A Christian has provision for it in going to the Lord Jesus and emptying himself of all mental loads and happily receiving in its stead 'rest', a condition that is an essential prerequisite for paying attention totally.

To put it simply, a Christian meta-love-counselor ought to spend time with the Lord before engaging a person in counseling. A minimum of 10 minutes is a suggestion. Each one has to decide on a comfortable period for this. Whatever may be your idea of prayer, this pre-counseling prayer should consist of three distinct stages. The first part is to deposit all your loads with the Lord, the second is to receive from Him the promised 'rest' and the third is for expressing your gratitude for the transaction. A heart filled with gratitude will be more at peace anywhere, anytime, doing anything good. A thankful heart has no complaints. A thankful heart is disposed to attend fully.

Be a person prepared enough to attend fully.

6. Interpathic oneness with the troubled person

Attending fully in that state of 'rested' mind and experiencing the abiding Jesus all around and within, the Meta-love-counselor moves closer to the troubled person in openness unusual to mere professionalism. Something more than professionalism takes hold of the counselor. At that state of being, the meta-love-counselor cannot afford to be a closed self-assuming professional technical expert. The meta-love-counselor becomes disposed to see and accept another human being without qualifying conditions. An irresistible sense of equality, which comes only from sharing in the atoning blood that flowed on Calvary, grips the meta-love-counselor and turns him into a channel of healing even as she/he experiences the pain of the counselee in pain. The counselor has to be a rested, comforted, healed person that he may offer to anyone in any sort of problem the same comfort he himself has received from the Father of all comfort. The counselor is comforted for this very purpose. That is the Christian met-love-counselor's anthem[146] (2 Cor. 1:3-4).

The counselor has to feel one in suffering with the suffering person and share the treasure of comfort vested in him. This precisely is the interpathic oneness. This counselor function of being one with the person in trouble, in understanding the expressed and unexpressed emotions, thoughts, pain and spiritual attitudes beyond words is not optional.

It is obligatory.

The Meta-love- counselor with such a disposition encounters no real barriers in personal relating. Nothing keeps him apart from the pain of the person in trouble. Such a counselor is able to touch the untouchable including the leper and AIDS sufferer. Such a counselor has no problem in identifying with the marginalized, maimed, ungainly, ugly and the despised. The counselor is intensely aware of the apparent background situations behind the experiences of this person. Nothing would cloud his vision and blind him to miss the butterfly in the caterpillar, the hidden saint in the sinner.

The love of his Master constrains him to reach out and be one with those who are in pain. Pain has no caste, color, creed, currency, distinctions. Pain anywhere on earth has the same caricature. The Meta-love- counselor's joy is the privilege to be of service to the least. The Meta-love-counselor of my perception is a saint as Paul saw and addressed the followers of Jesus in Corinth, Ephesus and Philippi and so on. Be a person who can totally identify physically, mentally and spiritually with the troubled. This is not over identifying and becoming stuck as in the ordinary genus of counseling.

7. Help the troubled person to discover himself in fresh light

The person you are trying to help has been living and trying to cope with his life in a manner he thought was the best under his circumstances. Obviously, he was faulty in his understanding and processing of his confusing circumstances as evidenced by the mess he is in. A paradigm shift is called for at this point. The m-l-counselor, having gained a reasonable bonding with the person, now needs to help him to get a hold of the apparent reality of his situation through gentle eliciting dialogue. That is not the end of it.

The m-l- counselor knows there is the truth behind every set of apparent realities.

It is the right time now for the crucial task of revealing the truth behind the troubling experiences. All that has been achieved in consolidating the relationship with the meta-love- counselor and the troubled person comes to have a great bearing at this point. It is the trust this troubled person has in the m-l-counselor which would let him take a tentative step in accepting the revelations of the truth that are before him. Seeing and accepting the truth and acknowledging the responsibility that something has to be done to be free from the grips of the prevailing suffering sets the person free and opens for appropriate action. "This is the truth of my situation. I need to be free from it to lead a contented life and for that I have to do what needs to be done, the sooner the better. I think I can trust this person who is helping me to see clearly the path ahead".

When the troubled person arrives at this conclusion further progress in the mending of the person's life begins to take off. There is self-discovery, discernment of truth and fresh hope at this point. From there on growth to wholeness and healing in Jesus becomes a possibility.

You need to be sure this happens in the provisions of your Master and the One who is in charge of the counseling that is in progress. You do not do anything by yourself; only be yourself as you are in your identity with the Lord Jesus in His wholeness and reflect His glorious presence. You need to share your transparent oneness in Jesus with this person in trouble. Be a help in discovering the truth.

8. Help the person to give up all burdens into the invigorating hands of Jesus

The person going through the experience of self-discovery is intensely aware of the burden of anxiety, fear, anger, guilt, self-pity, unforgiveness, self-condemnation, depressive and self-destructive thoughts, and in the process of counseling is mentally and spiritually prepared to unload all his burdens into the inviting hands of Jesus who says, 'Come to me, all you who are weary and burdened, and I will give you rest'.

The meta-love-counselor comes across a fresh hindrance here. Despite the mental and spiritual preparedness, the person in trouble is not familiar with this spiritually effective principle. The practical and physical application of this Christian ethos would encounter resistance from the uninitiated. Most people and especially those of us in the East have a hang up about philosophies like 'Karma'. We believe in doing things to receive something. Grace and undeserving favors is apprehensively looked at.

'Does that sort of thing happen?' People unfamiliar with the grace of our Lord Jesus Christ and the love of God and the fellowship of the Holy Spirit may doubt that. This is the juncture where the m-l-counselor can and should explain the depths of Jesus Christ and His love, His forgiveness, His compassion and the standing offer of His fellowship. He has firsthand experience of this from his Master.

Describe to the person how He forgives and accepts those who are stamped as 'sinners' by the public. Show how He lives and mingles with the least of men, how He is unbiased and impartial. Tell the person about His willingness to touch the untouchables, how He heals and gives new life even to dead people, how He rejects the hypocrisy of the holier-than-thou snobs in the community. Explain His distaste for rigidity and scorn for heartless religiosity but how He is ever ready to heal and comfort all who turn to Him. He helps the lame to their feet, gives light to the blind, releases those bound in guilt and in private sorrow. This Jesus is waiting to be invited in to abide in any one who cares to welcome Him.

Coming from a convicted and candid personal experience of the m-1-counselor in whom the person has invested his trust, what is heard and witnessed would be more readily appreciated. As faith germinates and trust blossoms the yield in blessings is plenty. Help the person to shed fear and accept the Lord of all comfort. A technician will never be able to do this. Be good at and teach the discipline of going to the giver.

9. Walk along with the person to the top

If you have proceeded carefully and in line with the love of Christ, you are in a reasonable setting to extend wholesome help to the person in pain. You have fully identified with the person and as a meta-love-counselor have fully seen that person's problems and have sensed the depth of his suffering. You have arrived at a level of oneness with the person in trouble. His life by now is an open book before you. By now, you have come to identification with that person emotionally, intellectually and spiritually. The person is comfortable with you and is open with you without pretension. He knows you will honor confidentiality in every stage of the counseling. He trusts you because of the fact who you are.

Now it is up to you to walk along with the troubled person until you lead him to the heights of his personal potential. It is like leading a person up a mountain in an arduous climbing. In your company he has the disposition to take on the upward journey. You as a counselor have led many up onto the top of similar mountains.

You know the way. The leading makes all the difference.

It should not be a pulling up from above or pushing up from beneath but it needs to be a side-by-side walking up holding hands and gently helping to go higher. It has to be a planned, systematic peaceful progression. It cannot be a hurried rush to reach the top. Restlessness is never a help for those who are seeking peace and freedom from troubling experiences. It only escalates the already complicated situation.

If the m-l-counselor is willing to walk the extra mile, this is the time to do it. Go along and reach the person in trouble to the top of his possibilities in Christ. At the mountain top let him exclaim lifting his hands in exultation, 'Ha, I have arrived. I have hope and peace now. The Lord is my rock and my refuge. 'Praise God'!

Be a companion in the upward journey.

10. Instill restful maintenance of spiritual heights

A person at the top of his possibilities might have qualms about being alone at the top. A person who has consolidated oneness with the Lord Jesus Christ would never be alone. 'Lo! I am with you always, till the end of the ages' is a categorical assurance for all time for all those who believe. Jesus is God who is there with each one of His children. Getting that closeness with Him is the secret to lasting and abiding peace wherever one may be, down in the trough or up on the crest.

Human personality consists of spirit, soul (mind) and body. All the three are mutually interactive and complimentary. Each interacts and influences each other as a 'whole' entity. Disturbances in mind and/or spirit can cause upsets/changes in the body and vice versa all around. Peace in the spirit can influence the mind and/or body to enter into peaceful states. Man relates to God through the spirit and derives peace and wholeness. Natural calming down of the body and mind would make this spiritual union easier.

Physical, mental and spiritual means should be designed and followed. The Psalms is an excellent book that gives practical instruction in this area. The meta-love-counselor should be of assistance to the person in trouble in discovering and practicing the principles from the experiences of the persons closer to God. 'Search me, O God and know my heart; test me and know my anxious thoughts[147] (Ps 139:23). You discern my going out and my lying down; ... ... Before a word is on my tongue you know it completely... ... Such knowledge is too wonderful for me[148] (Ps 139:3, 4, 6). Blessed is the man who does not walk in the counsel of the wicked or stand in the way of sinners or sit in the seat of mockers' 149 (Ps 1:1).

He said to me "You are my Son; today I have become your Father. As of me and I will make the nations your inheritance, the ends of the earth your possession"[150 159] (Ps 2:8). Look on me and answer, O LORD my God. Give light to my eyes, or I will sleep in death; ... ... I will sing to the LORD, for he has been good to me[150] (Ps 13:3, 6).

I said to the Lord "You are my Lord; apart from you I have no good thing"[151] (Ps 16:2). I love you O LORD, my strength. The LORD is my rock, my fortress and my deliverer; my God is my rock, in whom I take refuge[152] (Ps 18:1, 2). To you O LORD, I lift up my soul; in you I trust, O my God[153] (Ps 25:1). Blessed is he whose transgressions are forgiven, whose sins are covered.

Rejoice in the LORD and be glad, you righteous; sing, all you who are upright in heart![154] (Ps. 32:1, 11). LORD, have mercy on me; heal me, for I have sinned against you[155] (Ps 41:4). Be pleased O LORD to save me: O LORD, come quickly to help me[156] (Ps 40:13). As the deer pants for streams of water, so my soul pants for you, O God[157] (Ps 42:1).

'Have mercy on me, O God according to your unfailing love; according to your great compassion blot out my transgression. Wash away all my iniquity and cleanse me from my sin[158] (Ps 51:1, 2). Have mercy on me, O God, have mercy on me for in you my soul takes refuge'[159] (Ps 57:1).

'My soul finds rest in God alone; my salvation comes from Him. Find rest, O my soul, in God alone; my hope comes from Him. Pour out your hearts to Him, for God alone is our refuge[160] (Ps 62:1, 5, 8). You guide me with your counsel, and afterward you will take me into glory. My flesh and my heart may fail, but God is the strength of my heart and my portion forever'[161] (Ps 73: 24, 26).

'Hear O LORD and answer me, for I am poor and needy..... Guard my life... ....Have mercy on me... ... .Bring joy to your servant... ... .I lift up my soul... ... ...You are forgiving and good, O LORD. Teach me your way LORD and I will walk in your truth'[162] (Ps 86:1, 2, 3, 4, 5, 11).

The LORD is my shepherd; I shall not be in want... ... my cup overflows[163] (Ps 23:1, 5).

Abiding in the Lord is made easier through living by His Word. Be a practitioner and instructor in the art of maintaining true spiritual heights.

11. Receive, Release and Rejoice; the three R's of Christian counseling

All said and done at the end of the day, what Christian-Meta-love- counseling aims at is receiving and appropriating the grace of our Lord Jesus as sufficient for all our needs. A Christian M-l-counselor ought to be a person who is abundant in grace, endowed with grace to share it lavishly with those who are in need of it, and then leading them to the source of all grace and getting them connected to that source.

The function of all Christians is to lead the thirsty to the river and let them drink their fill and bring all others to the river of life.

> "Cause me to come to Thy River O Lord
>
> Cause me to drink from Thy River O Lord
>
> Cause me to live by Thy River O Lord
>
> Cause me to come, Cause me to drink,
> Cause me to Live."

Receive grace and wholeness from Jesus, release it to the troubled, and rejoice in grace and wholeness restored in the troubled. This is what I call the three R's of Christian counseling. What is received is released for blessing others. There is reason to rejoice in the selfless releasing.[165] "My cup runneth over", says David (Ps 23: 5). It is not hard to pour out from a cup that is full and running over.

To receive, release and rejoice one has to be relaxed, physically, mentally and spiritually. Great things begin to happen in that state of the body, mind and spirit. It is too idealistic to be true. Yet that is what happens when Christ Jesus abides in the believer. This is what we call abiding, the ultimate in man-Jesus relationship. Although abiding is a Johnanian concept, resting is very much an Old Testament concept among the faith warriors of those days. The most prominent among them was none other than King David.

His richly varied life is seen through his psalms which are a source to enjoy the calming experiences he had through seeking the Lord. Seeking, trusting, receiving from the Lord is a Christian way for increasing the Christ-awareness in the believer. It is an intentional turning of your spiritual eyes onto Jesus and staying tuned to listen to His tender words of peaceful wholeness. Christ in you is the hope of glory.

This is how God showed his love for us:[164] 'God sent his only Son into the world so we might live through him' (1 John 4, The Message).

PETAL-24

THE BASIC TENETS OF CHRISTIAN-META -LOVE -COUNSELING

1. COMMITMENT TO ALL IN AGAPE FRAME OF MIND.

DEEPLY ROOTED UNCONDITIONAL LOVE; EXPECTING NOTHING BACK.

The Christian Meta-love-counselor relates to all in an ambience of the Agape frame of love. This precludes the contention that no Christian Meta-love-counseling can transact in an environment devoid of Agape Love. A Christian Meta-love-counselor has no other environment to operate from. A CMLC (Christian Meta-love-counselor) has or should not have any other platform to act from. The presence of Christ in the Meta-love- counselor and the counselee in the course of counseling are one unit, interpathically bound in Agape. The ground for healing is ready and pre-readied even before the counseling process gets under way in the reflection of it in your being which manifests itself in the supreme Presence of the Holy Spirit in Jesus the ultimate healer.

2. The Meta-love-counselor is led by the principle that everyone is God's created entity and as such totally acceptable without judgment. There is no place for any type of discrimination. Christ came to minister to the needy, rejected, evildoers, tax collectors, prostitutes and the so called sinners by community standards. A meta-love-counselor never discriminates between poor and rich, criminals and Pharisees, cheaters and manipulators, drunkards, prostitutes, bribe takers and red tape villains, political crooks and con artists. It is by grace of God only that you are not in any of these groups. You have no mandate to reject anyone in word or deed.

Hm..., all said and done, not easy brother!

3. The word interpathy and all it stands for might create some sort of confusion and be a hurdle in the total understanding of Meta-love-counseling. Interpathy is way beyond empathy as Christian-Meta-love-counseling is from the ordinary counseling practice. Let me try to put it as simply as possible. Empathy is the intellectual understanding of the pain of a paining person. Interpathy is being in onement with the pain of the paining person. The difference is in knowing the pain and being in the pain. It smacks of over-identification in common counseling parlance. Impractical or impossible on the surface of it but not in the depths of it, as this is the constraining Love of Christ. I have personally gone through it in scores of time. Experiencing the overt rejection of the

Samaritan woman at the well by all except those who used her, Jesus' instant empowering of her by asking,[165] "Give Me a drink" John 4:7(NASB), is a beautiful example of interpathy.

4. A Christian Meta-love-counselor needs to declutter and dump all the mental content before even aspiring to be a Meta-love-counselor; an unbiased mind and an uncluttered consciousness are strict prerequisites in Meta-love-counseling. Cluttering is caused by simple irritations, anxieties, brooding, fears, doubts, anger, failures, gilt, unforgiveness, thoughts of getting even, vendetta, evil desires, covert plans to discredit, overt and covert rejections, inferior feelings, pushy agendas, loud gaff, pretended piety, and a whole lot of undesirable and unholy thoughts; not in agreement with the mind of Christ and definitely not those who are 'in-a-pharisaic-mode' of existence.

Let me give you a highly condensed alphabetic list of the areas; a Meta-love-counselor needs to get rid of, before becoming eligible for the humble ministry of healing., (Please get rid of some of the unneeded very human conditions that might be concealed in you, Without your realizing it; like:-

> *Addiction and Rehab, Anger, Anxiety, Bereavement, Body shaming, Boredom, Confusion, Critical, Depression, Dis-ease, Disgust, Doubting, Exasperation, Faith systems, Failures, Family, Frustrations, Generalized gloominess, Gratification drives, Grief, Haughty, Hypochondria, Insomnia, Laziness, Losses, Marriage complications, Miserly, Mood swings, Narcissism, Negativity,*

> *Obesity, Overactive, Persistence to perform, Perversions, Pessimism, Pride, Quick reactions, Relationships, Rejection, Religion, Revenge, Sex, Sinfulness, Shame, Students misguided, Superstition, Trauma, Unforgiveness, Uncaring, unthinking, Vendetta, Vexation, Vices, Vocation, Wasting, Weariness, Youth, Zealotry and so on ad infinitum; a few only from myriads of human conditions*

A Christian Meta-counselor needs to be a comforted person in sync with (2 Cor. 1:3-4). A counselor not experiencing the comfort that Christ offers is not competent to offer comfort to anyone for that matter. We know, we believe, and we experience the inexpressible joy of being in Him. One of the occupational hazards in Christian Meta-love-counseling, is that we may fall short of the expected 'level-of-being-in-Him'. The moment we doubt His assurances and our own experiences, we distort His image of Him that is within us. Occasional set-backs in these areas are not to be considered personal failures which are to be seen in the larger canvas that Jesus holds forth.

That is not any bizarre visualization. It does not depend on anything you do; on the contrary, it is the quality of His ubiquitous presence and the feeble reflection of His gloriously enormous powerful presence in you which turns out you to be an unimaginable healer under His wings!

The qualitative changes that normally happen in you as a loving being in a blessing-mode-of- existence, is nothing short of a miracle. We assume that miracles happen when man eases himself into a loving-blessing-mode-of existence. This is an existential possibility in Him who makes all things possible universally. From the counselor/helper/comforter's part it is only necessary to yield to the love of Christ which makes all impossible possible. Meta-love-counseling is that simple to turn into a blessing presence. In case you feel it is only a feeling and it will fade away; do not believe that feeling, ignore the earthquake, fire and storm, but listen to the gentle whisper.

"Be blessed, you are equipped and enabled to be a blessing presence"

Our personal Christian endowments are all givens and not cumbersome as one may fear. The list may appear formidable and impossible, but they are adorably simple when they come to happen to you in Him; abiding in Him.

Although said variously in different part of this book, let us take a simple consolidated look for clarity and emphasis which need to be exemplified in our Being.

It is all about 'Being';

> "Be holy as my heavenly Father is holy" Be Love as Christ is Love; Be Pure; Be Holy, Be Accepting; Be Humble; Be Gentle; Be Faithful; Be Good; Be Kind; Be Patient; Be tolerant; Be Self-controlled. Most of it is the fruit of the Spirit as you recognize. Personal purity and holiness are the keys to be a reflecting presence of His magnificence.

Along with that comes what transforms you to be a blessing to all those who sand in need of transformation; you functioning as a transcending tool in His hands; You just 'Be' what He equips you to 'BE'

be a Blessing, Be a Healing Presence in your interpathic resonance in His Grace.

Before I take leave of you from the petals of this flower, let me give you a few verses which keep influencing me in a big way:-

1. 1 Cor. 14:1. Follow the way of love and eagerly desire spiritual gifts especially the gift of prophecy- (*and counseling, added by me*)

   John 13:34; A new commandment I give you; love one another As I have loved you, so you must love one another.

2. Rom. 5:5. And hope does not disappoint us, because God has poured out His love into our hearts by the Holy Spirit, whom He has given us.

3. Rom. 8:35-39. Who shall separate us from the love of Christ? Shall trouble or hardship or persecution or famine or nakedness or danger or sword? As it is written:

   "For your sake we face death all
   day long,
   We are considered as sheep to be
   Slaughtered"

No in all these things we are conquerors through Him who loved us. For I am convinced that neither death, nor life, neither angels nor demons, neither the present nor the future, nor any powers, neither height nor depth nor anything else in all creation will be able to separate us from the love of God that is in Christ Jesus our Lord.

4. 1. John 4: 7-8. Dear friends, let us love one another, for love comes from God. Everyone who loves has been born of God and knows God. Whoever does not love does know God, because God is LOVE.

5. 1 John 5:20 We also know that the Son of God has come and has given us understanding, so that we may know Him who is true. And we are in Him who is true - even in His Son Jesus Christ. He is the true God and eternal life.

Printed in the United States
by Baker & Taylor Publisher Services